The Art of
HORARY
ASTROLOGY

Öner Döşer, AMA, ISAR CAP

Edited with a Preface by
BENJAMIN N. DYKES, PHD

The Cazimi Press
Minneapolis, Minnesota
2019

Published and printed in the United States of America

First American edition published by:
The Cazimi Press
Minneapolis, MN

© 2019 AstroArt Astroloji ve Danışmanlık Ltd. Şti.

All rights reserved. No part of this book may be reproduced, stored in an electronic retrieval system, or transmitted in any form or by any means, electronic, mechanical, graphical, recording or otherwise, without the written permission of the copyright holder.

Translation by:
Sibel Oltulu

Edited by:
Mustafa Konur, Sibel Oltulu, Sharon Knight, and Benjamin N. Dykes

Original design by:
Mustafa Konur
mustafakonur@gmail.com

First Printing (February 2017) by:
AstroArt Astroloji ve Danışmanlık Ltd. Şti.
Bağdat Cad. No. 284 Canoğlu Apt.
Kat: 3 Daire: 20 Kadıköy/İstanbul
Tel: 0216 386 73 96
www.astrolojiokulu.com
info@astrolojiokulu.com
Certificate No: 22202

ISBN-13: 978-1-934586-51-8

TABLE OF CONTENTS

PREFACE 5
INTRODUCTION: HORARY, A.K.A. *MESAIL*
  ("QUESTIONS") 1
1: CONSIDERATIONS BEFORE JUDGMENT 6
2: SIGNIFICATORS 30
3: MEANINGS OF HOUSES IN GENERAL, AND IN HORARY
   ASTROLOGY 53
4: SIGNS, COUNTRIES, REGIONS, CITIES, & PLACES 60
5: CLASSIFICATION OF THE SIGNS 75
6: PRACTICAL ADVICE ON ANSWERING HORARY
   QUESTIONS 78
7: EXAMPLE CHARTS 150

APPENDIX A: TABLE OF DIGNITIES 195
APPENDIX B: GLOSSARY 196
REFERENCES 208
ABOUT THE ASTROART ASTROLOGY SCHOOL 211

PREFACE

This book is part of a new series in support of the traditional astrology courses of the AstroArt Astrology School in Istanbul, headed by my friend and colleague Öner Döşer. It follows our successful release of his *Astrological Prediction* (2015), *Financial Significators* (2018), and *Professional Significators* (2018).

After a long career in Istanbul's oldest and most prestigious bazaar, Öner followed his heart and turned fully to astrology, soon becoming one of the leading astrologers in Turkey, with numerous television appearances and books to his credit. His Astrology School Publishing has released 14 well-received books, not to mention his own articles in international astrological publications. Since 2012 he has been the organizer of the highly successful International Astrology Days in Istanbul.

Öner Döşer blends traditional and modern techniques and attitudes. For example, for horary charts he uses Regiomontanus houses, but for certain techniques he focuses on whole signs. In terms of planets, he uses the three outers as well as Chiron. However, he grounds his work in traditional authors, such as Ptolemy, Dorotheus, Firmicus Maternus, Māshā'allāh, Sahl, Abū Ma'shar, Schoener, Lilly, and others. For this new series I have largely provided my own translations of the original source material (both current and forthcoming), with sentence numbers in boldface in the footnotes. In some cases, I have updated older translations to reflect my current thinking. I have also added a few comments of my own, prefaced with **BD**.

I know you will enjoy these succinct and helpful guides to astrological interpretation, and your chart reading will improve as a result.

Benjamin Dykes, 2019

INTRODUCTION: HORARY, A.K.A. *MESAIL* ("QUESTIONS")

Horary astrology, known in Ottoman Turkish as *mesail* ("questions" or "problems"), is a branch of astrology based on charts erected in order to make judgments on immediate questions. The astrologer erects the chart for the moment when he understands the question, and judges this chart. It is the most interesting branch of astrology because, when its rules are applied meticulously, it provides surprisingly correct predictions. It is an essential branch of astrology, which any student of traditional astrology should study.

Among the many scholars who made extensive studies of horary astrology are the following: Dorotheus, Māshā'allāh, Abū Ma'shar, Abū 'Alī al-Khayyāt, al-Tabarī, Sahl b. Bishr, 'Alī ibn Abī al-Rijāl, and in later periods Guido Bonatti and William Lilly in later periods.[1] Guido Bonatti (in Latin, *Bonatus*) is the most famous astrologer of the Medieval Age: he referred extensively to the works of the Arabic astrologers, and some contemporary astrologers follow him. But the legendary *Christian Astrology* by William Lilly in the 1600s was the most comprehensive book on astrology in the English language, and is still classed as one of the most important books on questions studied by traditional astrologers to date.

Astrology in the Ottoman State

This information on horary which became widespread in the 18th and 19th Centuries influenced some of the Ottoman astrolo-

---

[1] See the list of astrologers in Dykes's *The Book of the Nine Judges* (hereafter, *Judges*) pp. 6-7.

gers: Sadullah Efendi from Ankara,[2] who lived in the first half of the 19th Century, is one of them. A regent, head of the registry office, mufti, and poet, Sadullah Efendi was also a *munajjim* (astrologer, but especially in a governmental capacity) like his grandfather Sheikh Mustafa Efendi and his father, Aldulkerim Efendi.[3] He erected charts especially for questions he asked himself regarding his servants,[4] and from his articles in *Zayiçe Mecmuası* ("Magazine of Horoscopes") we can see that he made extensive studies related to employing his servants, determining the time for starting a journey, and for carrying out his daily work and obligations.[5] Through his connections with high government officers he made contact with other influential people in Istanbul, and through his wide circle of acquaintances he was supported by some influential people like the military commanders Izzet Pasha and Nafiz Pasha.[6] He also tried to teach his son Pertev how to prepare a calendar.[7]

We know that these *munajjims*, who had great knowledge of mathematics, astronomy, and astrology, also trained students. One of them was Mustafa Asim Bey, the Chief Munajjim between 1898 and 1901, and the father of Namik Kemal, the famous Ottoman poet. Many students studied under Mustafa Asim Bey, thanks to his vast knowledge of astronomy and astrology, as he was the master of his era. He recorded everything to the very minute, made his daily plans based on astrological aspects, and erected charts for the questions he received.[8]

As in many cultures, astrology was a part of daily life in the Ottoman state. The emphasis on astrology is evident both from the

---

[2] His full name was Mudarriszade Sadullah el-Ankaravi.
[3] Houlding and Döşer, p. 17.
[4] Koç, p. 50.
[5] Koç, p. 50.
[6] Koç, pp. 45-46.
[7] Koç, p. 41.
[8] Ayduz, pp. 236-39.

socio-cultural perspective and in view of intellectual history. In her postgraduate thesis, Gulcin Tunali Koç states: "As astrology is involved extensively in daily life, what it brought to socio-cultural history cannot be ignored, and astrology leads the way in intellectual history."[9]

Called by the Ottomans *ilm-i ahkam-i nujjum*,[10] astrology was divided into two branches: natural and judicial. Judicial astrology was then subdivided into three parts: *mevalid* (nativities), *mesail* (questions or horary), and *ihtiriyat* (elections or inceptions). Casting charts for the moment in order to find lost items or missing people, and giving information on various situations and people, were typical for questions: so, "questions" is the name of both the area we are studying here and the very problems posed to the astrologer.[11] Elections or inceptions were used for determining the best time to initiate an action, and of course nativities determined the characteristics and destiny of natives based on the natal chart.[12]

From the 15th Century to the 20th, Chief Munajjims wielded great power in the Ottoman Empire. The Chief Munajjim was meticulously selected from among the palace astrologers who attended the classical *madrasah* or school, and were well trained in astronomy and astrology. This position became official during the period of Beyazit (r. 1389-1402), and came to end in 1924 with the 37th and last Chief Munajjim, Huseyin Hilmi Efendi.

On a personal note, learning that the 35th Chief Munajjim, Seyyid Mehmed Arif Efendi, was a maternal relative (the father-in-law of my mother's aunt) was both surprising and thrilling news. Arif Kaman, a senior member of our family, who was named after his

---

[9] Koç, p. 50.
[10] **BD**: This is directly from Arabic, and means, "the science of the judgments of the stars."
[11] Ayduz, p. 50.
[12] Ayduz, p. 105.

grandfather, told me he had some booklets, seals, and medals that belonged to his grandfather. One of my cousins arranged a family gathering and I visited them before publishing a version of this book on horary in Turkish.

Seyyid Mehmed Arif Efendi (hereafter, Seyyid Mehmed), who served as the Chief Munajjim in the palace between 1903 and 1909, was born in September 1853 and died in 1940. He was buried in Eyup Cemetery. As he was born in the city of Izmit, one of the streets in Izmit is named after him. During his career as a Chief Munajjim, he bought a mansion in the Suleymaniye district of Istanbul so as to be close to the palace. My relative Arif also reported from his father that Seyyid Mehmed was trilingual, also speaking Arabic and Persian. He was a productive man who worked across many disciplines, spending days on calculations in his library where he also wrote several books. While he was alive, his family gifted his works to the Islamic Arts Museum. Some are currently in Suleymaniye Library, and some in the Beyazit library. I hope one day to research these books and make a compilation of them.

Seyyid Mehmed took great efforts to act at propitious times, which is why he always cast electional charts for new ventures and arrangements in daily life, such as the time to go to his cottage, buying new garments, or putting them on. He prepared the nativities of his children and told them what was fated for them. For instance, he told his son Sacit (Arif's father), that he would not achieve high status, but neither would he be disgraced. He would be neither very happy nor very unhappy and would have an average life. He also predicted his time of his death, and told his family to be prepared on a certain day and time. Of course, no one in the family understood what he had prepared them for, until they were invited to their father's house. When they arrived, they realized why their father had told them to be there at that specific time.

Arif carefully kept some things left by his grandfather, including a photograph of him in his official uniform. Arif and another cousin kept the medals, which are on the breast of his caftan in this photograph; this caftan was exhibited in a museum. Another of Arif's cousins kept his professional license. Arif also showed me the official seals used by Seyyid Mehmed during his career as a Chief Munajjim. One of them, on which is written *es-Seyyid Mehmed Arif*, is illustrated in Ayduz's thesis,[13] which is on the Chief Munajjims in the Ottoman Empire.

Let's return to the present day...

In addition to the leading astrologers in Europe and America, an increasing number of astrologers in Turkey are now studying horary astrology. This book is the result of numerous notes I compiled for our horary classes at the AstroArt School of Astrology in Istanbul, which we have held for the past decade. (See the end of this book for more.) I hope this book will be beneficial for all readers who want to learn horary astrology.

---

[13] See the Appendix in Ayduz, "Documents and Photographs."

1: CONSIDERATIONS BEFORE JUDGMENT

The works we have inherited from the ancient astrologers inform us as to various points that should be considered when making judgments. William Lilly's *Christian Astrology* is the ideal guide on this issue. The considerations include examining the planetary lord of the hour for the question, whether the first or last degrees of a sign are rising, whether the Moon is in the last degrees of a sign, if she is in the burned path or *"via combusta,"* void in course, whether Saturn is in the 7th or 10th house of the chart, and whether or not the lord of the 7th is afflicted.

In this chapter, these considerations will be illustrated using example charts. Let's begin with how to erect the horary chart, based on the correct moment and place.

For which time and place should we erect the chart?

Since ancient times, many ideas have been suggested as to which time and place should be used for erecting a horary chart. Some of the Arabic astrologers suggested using the time and place where the querent actually meets with the astrologer, while others claimed we should use the moment when querent asks the question of the astrologer.

The majority of contemporary astrologers prefer erecting the chart for the moment they receive and understand the question, using their own location. The astrologer should be sure to perfectly understand what the querent is asking, in order to erect a chart.

Even if the question is received via e-mail or physical mail, the moment of the question is when the astrologer reads and understands what the querent is asking. The astrologer erects the chart based on the coordinates of where *he*, the astrologer, is. It is optional to erect the chart of the moment when the question is asked, although this chart is not used in judgment; it may reflect the querent's own environment.

Some of the ancient astrologers claimed that an astrologer should not answer his own questions, as he may not be objective when answering them. However, Lilly does not agree with the ancients on this issue. He answered his own questions and published the results in *Christian Astrology*.

Since ancient times, the masters of horary astrology warned their successors about features of the chart which should be considered before and while judging it. They developed rules so that the astrologer would not be misled or misinformed, would not misjudge and feel ashamed, and would not waste time on useless questions. A valid horary chart is called "radical."[14]

Is the chart radical?

To determine whether a question is radical, some factors should be considered. Lilly recommends we consider the harmony between the lords of the planetary hour and the Ascendant. He proposed three methods:

1. If the same planet is both the lord of the hour and the lord of the Ascendant, the question is radical. In the chart below (see Figure 1), the Sun is the lord of the Ascendant and the question is asked at the hour of the Sun, so he is also the lord of the hour.
2. If a planet is both the lord of the hour and one of the triplicity lords of the Ascendant, the question is radical. In Figure 2 below, Taurus is rising and its lord of the hour Mars is also one of the triplicity lords of Taurus. I person-

---

[14] **BD**: Literally, this means "rooted" (Lat. *radicalis*), and means that the question has a proper "foundation." It is a kind of celestial indication that one may proceed on a sure footing.

ally believe that the proximity between the lord of the hour (Mars) and the degree of the Ascendant is also important.

3. The lord of the hour and Ascendant could be of the same temperament. In Figure 3 below, both the rising sign Leo and the lord of the hour Mars, are choleric (hot and dry). Consequently, this question is radical as per Lilly's criteria.

One might also consider a chart radical if the Moon is in a close aspect with the lord of the hour, or if the lord of the hour has a close aspect with the degree of the Ascendant.

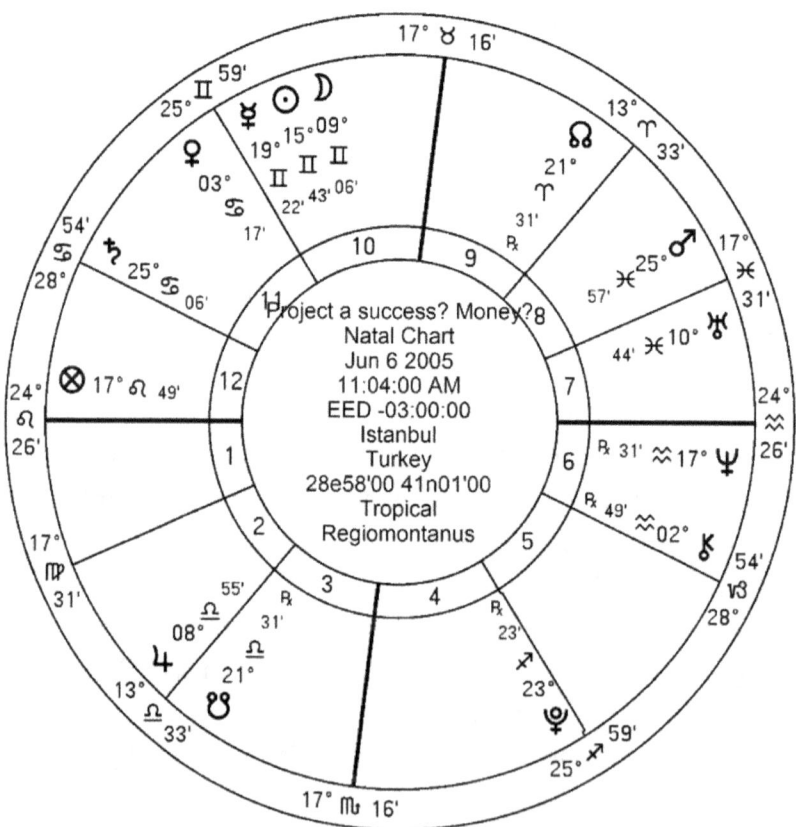

Figure 1: Will this project be a success? Will I get my money?

1: Considerations Before Judgment

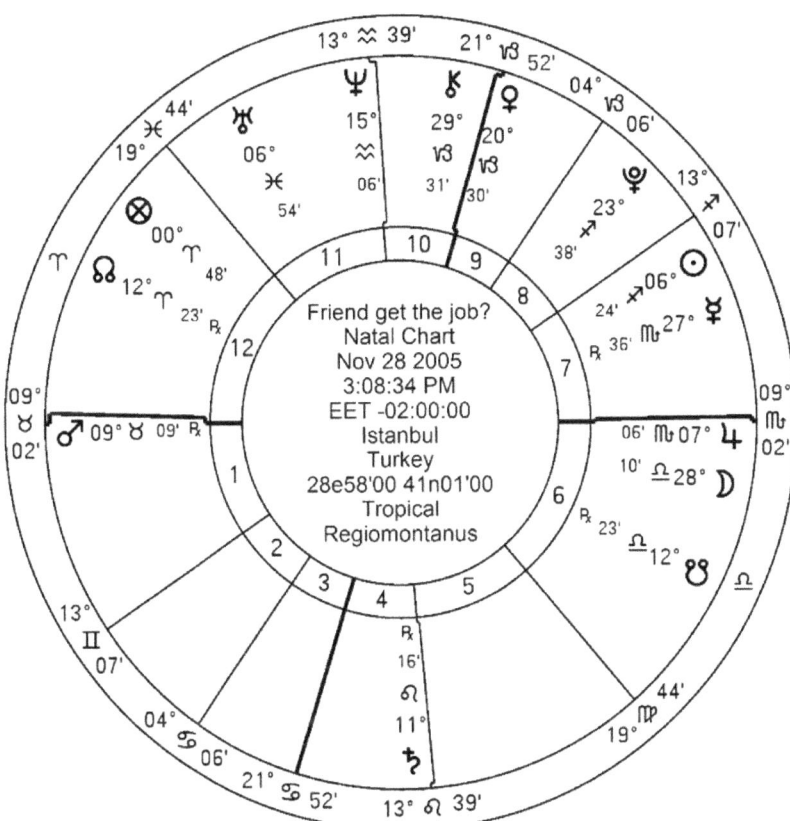

Figure 2: Will my friend get the job she wants?

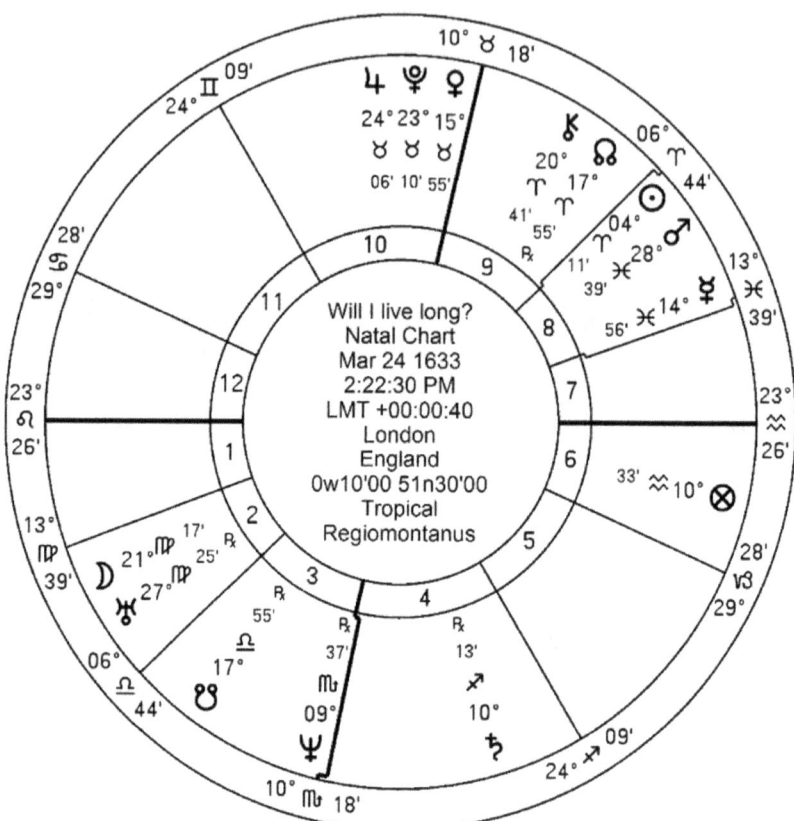

Figure 3: Will I live long?

Sue Ward, a researcher of Lilly's works and a horary astrologer, points out that ten example charts in *Christian Astrology* do not match the above-mentioned criteria. She also states that Lilly did not strictly observe the harmony between the lord of the hour and the Ascendant: in eight out of ten example charts which were not otherwise radical, the following factors were observed:

1. Lord of the hour in one of the angular houses.
2. Lord of the hour in the house of the quaesited.[15]
3. Lord of the hour is the natural or accidental lord of the matter.[16]
4. Lord of the hour having triplicity rulership in the rising sign.

Many contemporary astrologers, including myself, do not apply the lord of the hour criteria. In my opinion, when judging a horary chart we should first of all see if the chart actually fits the question's circumstances: it should tell the story of the question. In this regard, I believe that the factors mentioned below are important:

- Does the Ascendant or a planet close to it describe the querent, and tell us about the situation?
- Are the houses and signs where the luminaries placed, in accord with the question?

Let's examine the chart below with Aquarius rising and Neptune close to the degree of the Ascendant (Figure 4). The querent was an idealist (Aquarius) and there were some dubious issues (Neptune) related to his career. He was an assistant general manager, and his CEO was trying to pull the rug out from under him, as he saw the querent as a rival. At the time of the question the Sun, the lord of the 7th (open enemies) was in the 12th (behind-the-scenes

---

[15] **BD**: The "quaesited" or "quesited" means "the thing asked about": for example, if the question is about children, the house of the quaesited is the 5th. See Chapter 2 below.

[16] **BD**: The natural lord is a planet which indicates a matter through its own nature, such as Venus naturally indicating matters of love. The accidental lord indicates the matter because it rules the topic by house: if the question was about a marriage, the lord of the 7th would be its accidental lord, no matter which planet it was. So, the situation here would exist if the lord of the hour for a question about love was either Venus or the lord of the 7th.

acts). As the Sun represents managers, the Sun's position confirmed that the question is radical.

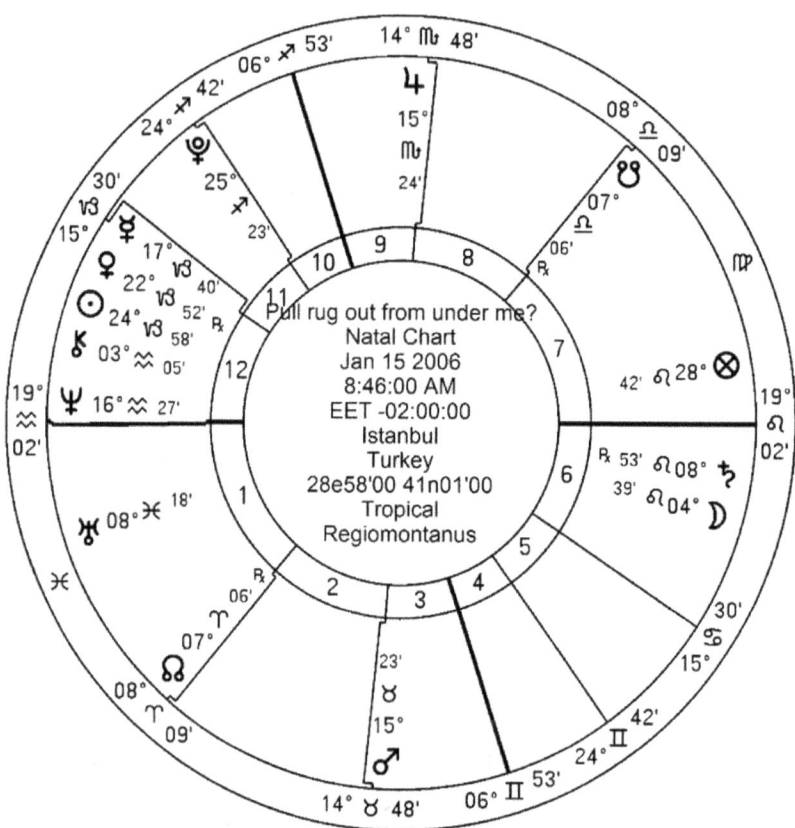

Figure 4: Will he pull the rug out from under me?

In another example below (Figure 5), the Sun is placed in the house that is related to the question. The question is about a business with friends, and the querent was in a catering business with his friends. The Sun is in the 11th (the house of friends), but as the lord of the Ascendant he represents the querent; the other two planets (Mercury and Saturn) represent the friends and business partners. When I asked the querent if one of his friends was staid, somber, and slow (Saturn) while the other was active, talkative, and skillful (Mercury), he confirmed it was the case.

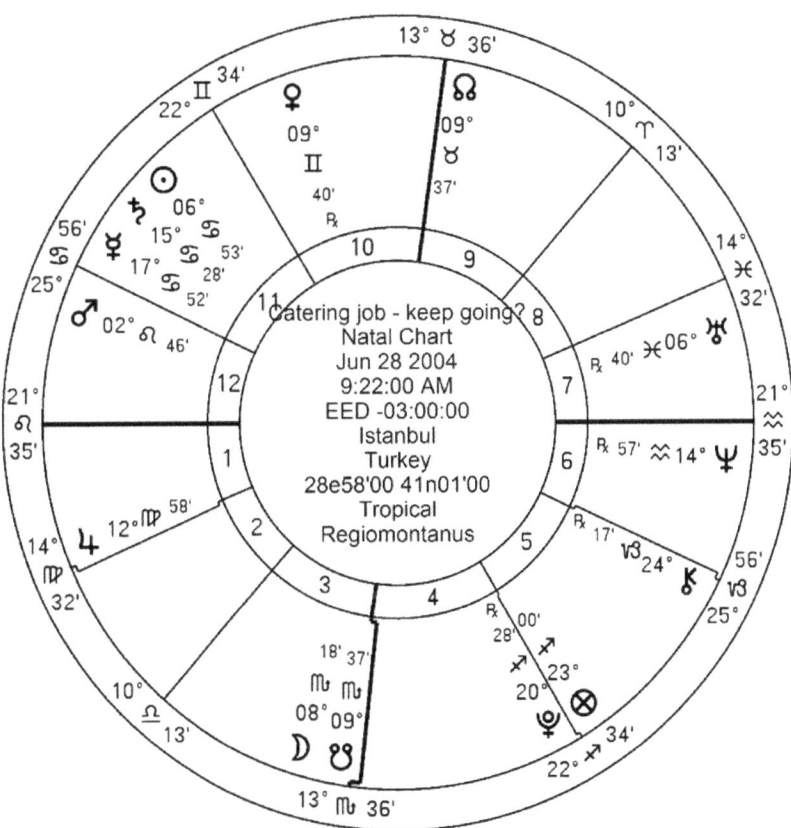

Figure 5: Will the catering job with my friends keep going?

If any of the planets in the querent's nativity are close to the degree of the Ascendant of the question, the question is radical. In the chart erected for Figure 5, Jupiter is at 12° Virgo. In the querent's nativity 12° Virgo is rising, so it coincides with Jupiter's degree in the horary chart (see Figure 6). The Midheaven of the nativity is on 9° Gemini, and this degree in the question has Venus on it, representing the querent's future and career, as she is the lord of the 10th house of the question. There are other connections between the two charts, but these two are important as they match the same degrees exactly.

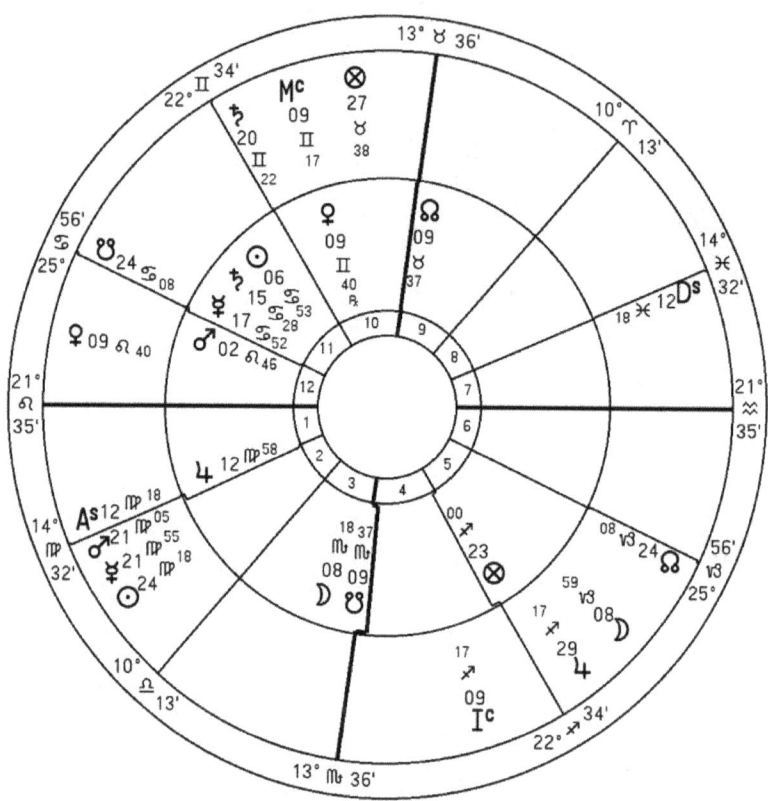

Figure 6: Will the catering job with my friends keep going? (Outer circle: querent's nativity, Sept 17, 1972, 5:50 AM, Istanbul, Turkey)

In a horary chart the sign and house wherein the Moon is placed, relates to the question in the querent's mind, namely what the querent is thinking about at that moment.[17] So, the house of the Moon should be considered for determining the radicality of the question.

---

[17] Barclay, p. 29.

In the chart below (Figure 7), the Moon is in Cancer, in the last degrees of the 3rd house and close to the 4th house, and is the lord of the 4th house. This alignment makes it a radical chart, as Cancer and the 4th house are related to issues of the home.

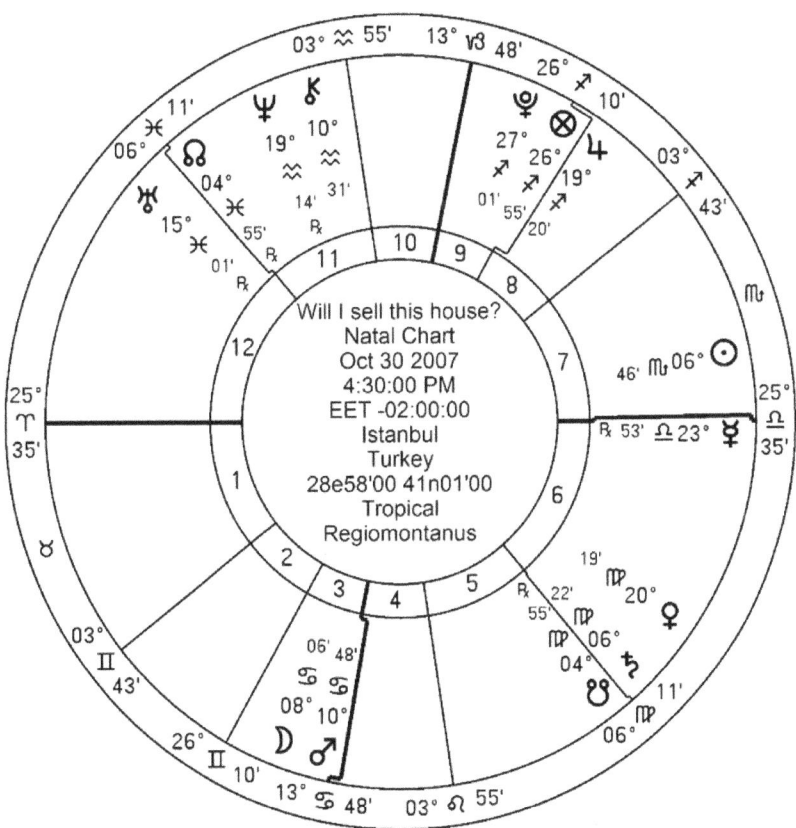

Figure 7: Will I sell this house?

The Moon's placement in the chart points out the "real" thoughts of the querent. The overt question may be about (say) the partner, but the intention behind it may be related to financial security. In Figure 8 below, Saturn is in the 2nd, indicating the querent's finances. The Moon, as lord of the 2nd house, represents the querent's finances and is in the 8th house, in Capricorn. This indicates that the querent is financially dependent on the quaesited (the partner's money) and had some expectations from him. The querent is overtly asking if his partner will return, but really wants to know if he will get any financial support from the partner.

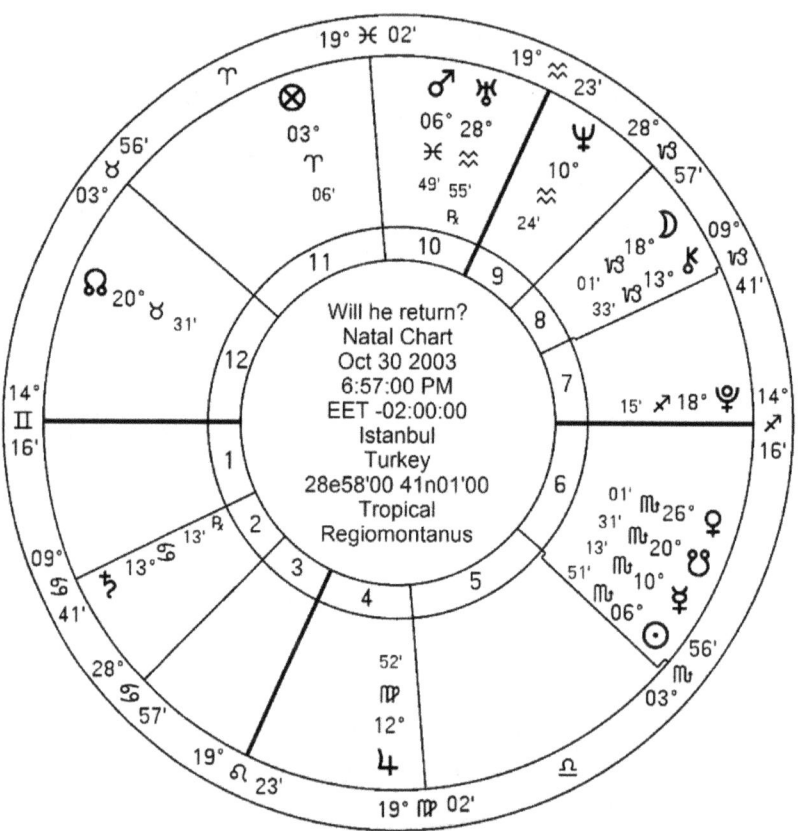

Figure 8: Will he return?

If the Moon's last aspect shows a recent event relating to the querent, the question is radical. In Figure 8 above, the Moon's last aspect was her opposition with Saturn. As the couple separated before the question, the Moon separating from Saturn also shows this separation. This proves that the question is radical.

There are also two points to consider in judgments:
- Is the querent interested in the question, both emotionally and physically?
- Is the question meaningful?

Some questions are not directly related to the querent's life, and sometimes querents ask questions which have no practical importance. Many horary astrologers refuse to answer such questions, as they are a waste of time and effort. The astrologer is not obliged to accept and answer any and all types of questions!

Early or late degrees on the Ascendant

If the first 3° of any sign are rising at the time of the question, then it is too early to make a judgment. If the sign on the Ascendant is one of the fastest signs,[18] it is too early to give an opinion on that issue because the issue has not yet been properly formed: the querent needs to have more information about it, or the events will not proceed to an end. There are still unforeseen events or people that may impinge on the outcome, so the resolution to the question is not yet fixed. Some additional changes may make the question useless later on. If additional changes occur, the question may be asked a second time. It may also indicate that the querent is trying to test or cheat the astrologer. Or, the question may just be a spontaneous one, asked on the fly, or not fixed yet.

On early degrees rising, Lilly states: "When either 0 degrees, or the first or second degrees of a Sign ascend (especially in Signs of short ascensions, *viz.* Capricorn, Aquarius, Pisces, Aries, Taurus, Gemini, you may not venture judgement, unless the Querent be

---

[18] **BD**: The fast, or "crooked" signs in the northern hemisphere are from Capricorn through Gemini, and the fastest among them are Pisces and Aries. In the southern hemisphere the fast signs are from Cancer through Sagittarius, and the fastest among them are Virgo and Libra.

very young, and his corporature, complexion and moles or scars of his body agree with the quality of the Sign ascending."[19]

If the last 3° of a sign are rising, then it is too late to ask that question. Some things are about to culminate and some changes are about to occur in the querent's life. Late degrees rising may also indicate the question has been solved or the matter is already determined. There is nothing that the querent can do to effect the situation. Or, some conditions may have changed, of which the querent is unaware. Late degrees may also indicate the querent may be trying to test or cheat the astrologer.

Lilly says about the last degrees of a sign rising: "If 27, 28, or 29 degrees ascend of any Sign, it's no ways safe to give judgement, except the Querent be in years corresponding to the number of degrees ascending; or unless the Figure be set upon a time certain, *viz.* a man went away or fled at such a time precise; here you may judge, because it's no propounded question."[20] According to Lilly, it is not safe to judge "when the Moon is in the later degrees of a Sign, especially in Gemini, Scorpio, or Capricorn; or as some say, when she is in *Via Combusta*, which is, when she is in the last 15 degrees of Libra or the first 15 degrees of Scorpio."[21]

According to Bonatti, as the latest degrees of a sign belong to the malefics, those degrees contain unfavorability.[22]

According to Olivia Barclay, 27° – 29° degrees of a sign rising indicate despair.[23]

According to Goldstein-Jacobson, the 29th degree of any sign is the critical degree or the crisis degree. There is an eagerness for

---

[19] Lilly, p. 122.
[20] Lilly, p. 122.
[21] Lilly, p. 122.
[22] Bonatti, Tr. II.2, Ch. 14 (pp. 64-65).
[23] Barclay, p. 124.

entering into the next sign, or one feels things are coming to an end.[24]

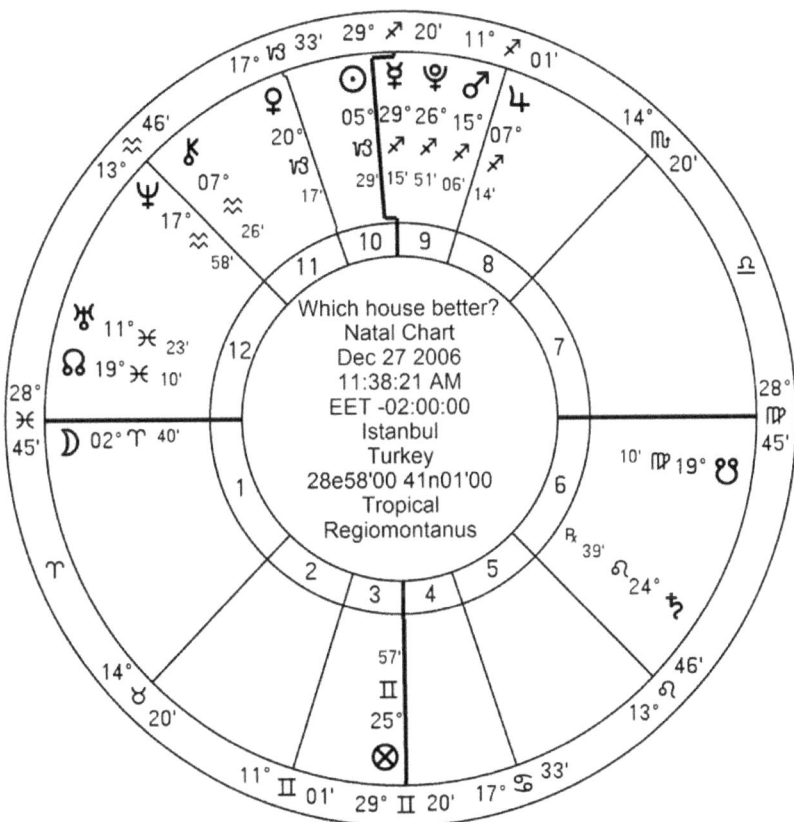

Figure 9: Which house is more beneficial?

From my point of view, having the last degrees of a sign on the Ascendant at the moment of the question is not a negative thing. However, we may think that some matters are about to culminate, or the decision is made but the astrologer is being asked for confirmation. In Figure 9 above, 28° Pisces is on the Ascendant. After I received the question, I told the querent that the decision was al-

---

[24] Goldstein-Jacobson, p. 53.

ready made and wouldn't be changed, and that he would soon take action. (Pisces is about to end and Aries will soon be rising; moreover, the Moon is already in Aries, as also in the querent's nativity.) This the querent confirmed. Here is an interesting detail about the querent: the natal Sun is at 27° Pisces and the natal Moon at 2° Aries: that is, the degree of the Ascendant of the question is in conjunction with the querent's natal Sun, while the Moon in the question is in conjunction with his natal Moon. This again shows us that nothing is coincidence.

The burned path or *via combusta* (15° Libra - 15° Scorpio)

When the Moon is between 15° Libra and 15° Scorpio , she is in the "burned path." This indicates that there will be some losses or difficulties related to the querent or the quaesited. Some astrologers claim that the Ascendant, its lord, or the main significators being in the burned path also bring the same results.

This is one of the most misunderstood rules among the considerations before judgment. In ancient times, when the Sun was transiting in Scorpio he was among some malefic stars of the nature of Mars and Saturn, which was perceived as a malefic and destructive situation. However, due to the precession of the ecliptic, the projections of the stars on the zodiac have changed since Ptolemy's period (the 2nd Century AD); now the malefic stars are not within these degrees. Consequently, contemporary astrologers do not pay attention to this rule. Some contemporary astrologers who pay attention to the burned path assume that it reflects the unpredictable fiery effect of Uranus, Mars, and Saturn, indicating illness, danger, fear, restriction and death. It is also related to death due to high fever.

According to some ancient astrologers like Dorotheus (who lived around the time of Ptolemy), the Moon degenerates and becomes inactive in the burned path.²⁵ Moreover, any significator in the burned path also becomes inactive so that it cannot work for the benefit of the person it signifies.

On the other hand, according to Anthony Louis, a planet which is conjoined with Spica (one of the fixed stars of a benefic nature which does lie in the burned path, and displays the character of Venus-Mars) within 1°, "participates in [Spica's] success and good fortune."²⁶

Some astrologers claimed that the Moon in the burned path prevents the judgment of the question. However, William Lilly did not advise actually canceling the judgment in such a case.²⁷ As Olivia Barclay also reminds us, some past astrologers like Henry Coley stated that the Ascendant in the burned path is not a stricture at all, and such a chart may be judged.²⁸

According to Barbara Watters, a contemporary astrologer, the Moon in the burned path resembles a Moon-Uranus connection: the course of events changes suddenly, unexpectedly, and unpredictably. She states that such a Moon brings wars, violence, accidents, disasters, the sudden death of the people in question, and damage to the quaesited's wealth.²⁹

Sue Ward states that "the Moon in the Via Combusta can show many things: fear, illness, death, hidden matters and imprisonment being some."³⁰

I personally think that the Moon's or another's placement within the burned path is not a critical element, although it may represent some negative developments about the querent or the question.

---

[25] Dorotheus, Ch. V.6, **12**.
[26] Louis, pp. 64, 165.
[27] Lilly, p. 122.
[28] Barclay, p. 124.
[29] Watters, pp. 14-15.
[30] Ward, *Considerations*.

Emptiness of course or void in course

When the Moon is void in course, it means that she makes no more major aspects to other planets before she leaves a sign. Bonatti recommends that we "look at the Moon when she is void in course: because then she signifies impediment, and that the matter the question was about…will not come to a good end, and the matter will be annulled, and it will not come to be nor be completed for the one wishing to do it; and that the querent will return from it empty-handed and likewise disgraced and impeded."[31] Success will only be obtained through hard work, and dealing with problems and sorrows. However, if the lord of the Ascendant or the significator of the quaesited is in a good position, there will be some obstructions but the result will not be that bad.

William Lilly says that the Moon is void in course if she does not apply to any other planet while within her current sign, after separating from her most recent aspect.[32] On the other hand, emptiness or being void is not limited to the boundaries of the sign she is in: if the Moon is in the last degrees of a sign and does not have any aspect within the same sign, but upon entering the next sign there is a planet with the orbs of an aspect, then she is not void in course. (However, Lilly does state that being burned or "combust" is limited to the boundaries of the sign.)[33]

In Lilly's method, the Moon may be void in course in any degree of the sign she is in because, starting with the 6th minute of arc after she separates from her latest aspect, she is void until she is within the orb of the planet with which she will make her next aspect. So, the Moon or another planet is not void if it she within the orb of the planet she will apply to, even if that other planet is in

---

[31] Bonatti, Tr. V, Consideration 19 (p. 285).
[32] Lilly, p. 112. That is, she must not apply within even orbs. See the example of the Moon and Saturn below, where being within orbs means she is not void.
[33] Lilly, p. 113.

the last degrees of a sign. For instance, let's assume that the Moon is at 29° Aquarius and Saturn at 1° Taurus. In this case the Moon is not void because she applies within the orb of sextile to Saturn in Taurus.[34]

According to Sue Ward, the Moon is not void in course if she is contacting another planet through their joint moieties, whether that aspect perfects in that current sign or in the next one.[35]

Most contemporary astrologers do not agree on this issue, as they limit the void course to the time when she exits the sign she is in. For instance, if the Moon is at 26° Pisces and void in course (i.e., not applying by a major aspect), she is void until entering Aries. Even if the Moon is within the orb of conjunction with another planet in the first degrees of Aries, she is still void in course. (Burning or combustion is also not limited by the boundaries of a single sign. For instance, when the Moon is at 26° Pisces and the Sun at 0°Aries, the Moon is still burned because burning is a relation to the Sun, not a sign. She will be even more affected as she gets closer to the Sun.)

According to Lilly, when the Moon is void in course the question seldom goes "handsomely forward"; nothing happens.[36] However, she can perform well if she is void in Cancer, Taurus, Sagittarius or Pisces, as these signs are dignities of Venus and Jupiter.[37] On the other hand, negative outcomes are likely in Gemini, Scorpio, or Capricorn: Lilly states that the question seldom has a good result in such circumstances. Again, when the Moon is void in course and the other main significators are not strong, difficulties are likely, although a positive outcome may still manifest when she is in Taurus, Cancer, Sagittarius, or Pisces. At any rate, a void in course

---

[34] Lilly, p. 471. **BD**: Although the Moon is in the last degree of her sign, Lilly considers her to be applying to Saturn in the first degree of his own sign.
[35] Ward, *Considerations*.
[36] Lilly, p. 112.
[37] Lilly, p. 122.

Moon means "there's no great hopes of the Question propounded."[38]

Some contemporary astrologers think that there is no need to worry as "nothing happens" when the Moon is void in course, or that there is nothing that the querent can do.[39] The aspects which the Moon makes within a single day, represents daily changes. Therefore, if the Moon does not make any aspect, then nothing changes in the course of events. Some astrologers like Goldstein-Jacobson, McEvers, and Derek Appleby, state that the querent should not worry about the question if they are asked when the Moon is void in course.[40]

From my point of view, a void in course Moon is not totally negative. If the other significators of the chart are strong, the event takes place but with some delays and difficulties. If the question is about a missing person or object, a void in course Moon indicates that the person or object will come back. Other significators being void in course also represent the same thing. Consequently, questions asked when something is void in course are radical and may be judged. However, the events may not become clear, and may not reach a solution.

The Moon in late degrees

According to Lilly, it is not safe to judge when the Moon is in the later degrees of a sign, especially in Gemini, Scorpio and Capricorn, because Gemini is the twelfth sign from Cancer (her sign), and Scorpio and Capricorn are ruled by the malefics.[41] Dorotheus also says that since the latest degrees of a sign are the bounds or terms typically ruled by the malefics, and as the Moon is not at

---

[38] Lilly, p. 299.
[39] Barclay, p. 124.
[40] Appleby, pp. 16-18.
[41] Lilly, p. 122.

ease in the signs of malefics, she is not at ease at the last degrees, either.[42]

I personally think that the Moon in the last degrees of a sign indicate that something is about to come to an end. If the Moon is in the signs just mentioned (Gemini, Scorpio, and Capricorn), the querent is having difficulties in completing matters, and experiencing a crisis. If the Moon is about to enter a sign where she feels comfortable, the conditions will soon change in a positive way.

Saturn in the 7th house or in other angular houses

This condition restricts both ancient and contemporary astrologers, as the 7th house is the house of consultation: it represents the astrologer who receives the question (when the question is not otherwise specifically about a 7th house matter). Some astrologers claim that Pluto in the 7th creates negative influences just as Saturn does.

If the lord of the 7th is afflicted, the astrologer may be in a difficult situation and have difficulty answering the question. He may have erected the wrong horary chart or made a mistake in calculation. If the lord of the 7th is retrograde, the astrologer should review the question and guard against a possible mistake. Some astrologers claim that the question should not be judged at all when the 7th house is afflicted, because the querent may not be satisfied with the answer and the astrologer may encounter some problems.

As Saturn is related to delays, it may take a long time for the astrologer to answer the question. The astrologer may make a poor judgment because Saturn may indicate a narrow point of view. According to Lilly, Saturn in the 7th house either corrupts the judgment of the astrologer or is a sign that "the matter propound-

---

[42] Dorotheus, Ch. V.6, **13**.

ed will come from one misfortune to another."[43] He adds: "The Lord of the seventh unfortunate, or in his fall, or in Terms of the infortunes, the *Artist* [sc. the astrologer] shall scarce give a solid judgment."[44] According to Lilly, if Saturn is in the Ascendant, especially retrograde, the matter of that question seldom or never comes to good. Lilly also states that when Saturn, Mars, or the South Node is peregrine or unfortunate in the 10th, the astrologer will hardly get any credit by answering that question.[45]

According to Lee Lehman, when planets are in the house pertaining to the question, they give information about its condition or people connected with it: "For instance, when Saturn is in the 7th House in a chart for a question about buying a property, it can simply indicate that the owners are old people."[46] According to Lehman, when Saturn is in the 10th house in a question which is not related to the 10th, the astrologer's reputation may be besmirched.[47]

Olivia Barclay notes that when Saturn is in the 1st house and retrograde, the matter seldom or never comes to good, but this is not an obstacle to reading the chart.[48]

If Saturn is in dignity by sign, exaltation, or triplicity, the problem related to the house he is in will be lessened. A malefic in its sign or exaltation, is better than a benefic which is retrograde and afflicted (unless it is afflicted due to another malefic).

In my view, Saturn in one of the angular houses at the moment of the question represents challenges for the querent. When I see Saturn in one of them, especially in the 7th, I do not hesitate to answer the question: I may be cautious and attentive, but I do not

---

[43] Lilly, p. 123.
[44] Lilly, p. 123.
[45] Lilly, p. 298.
[46] Lehman, p. 27.
[47] Lehman, pp. 27-28.
[48] Barclay, p. 125.

give up. Besides, if the question is about marriage and relations, the 7th house and its lord will actually represent the partner—that is, the quaesited—not the astrologer.

How to proceed in judgment?

We emphasized that we should check as to whether the question is radical before making a judgment. When we start analyzing the chart prior to making a judgment, first we need to determine the correct significators.

After correctly determining the significators, it is important to see the strength of these significators. This calculation is shown in William Lilly's *Table of Essential Dignities*.[49]

Next, examine the major aspects between the main significators. See if a third planet had an aspect with one or both of the significators, and if there is reception and/or an antiscial relationship between the significators.

Then the Moon's aspects in her current sign should be determined and noted down. The Moon's aspects with the main significators and other planets are crucial.

If the Moon aspects the cusp of the 4th house, or any planets in the 4th, these should also be examined because this aspect determines the outcome of events.

In addition to the antiscia of the main significators, the antiscion of the Moon should be determined.

Next, see if any fixed star is in conjunction with the main significator or the Moon.

Any Lots (sometimes incorrectly called "Arabic Parts") which are related to the question must also be determined.

In addition to the main significators, the planet which naturally represents the quaesited or the object needs to be determined. For instance, in a question about finding lost jewelry, we should con-

---

[49] Lilly, p. 104. **BD**: See Appendix A below.

sider the sign and house where Venus is, and the aspects she makes.

Answering more than one question through a single chart

In a horary chart more than one question may be answered, as we see in William Lilly's *Christian Astrology* (see Figure 10).[50] Here the question was from a military officer, *"if the querent will live long"*; but through this same chart Lilly answered other questions such as "In which part of the world shall I be successful?" and "What part of my life will be most fortunate?"

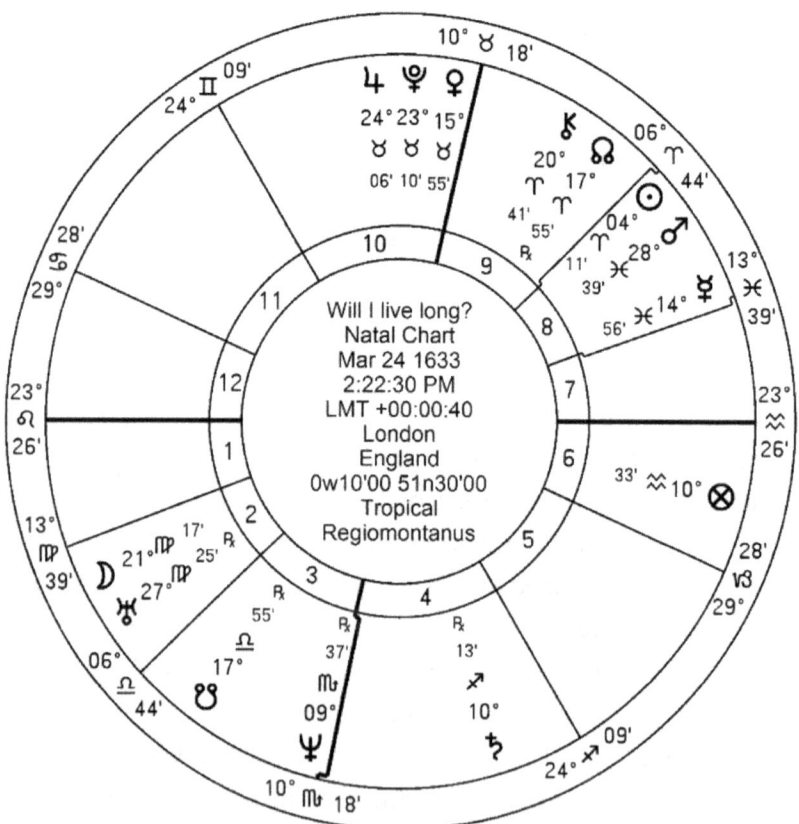

Figure 10: Will I live long?

---

[50] Lilly, p. 135.

1: Considerations Before Judgment

I also follow the same method. The questions in Figure 11 below were "Shall my project be successful? Shall I get my money?" These questions are interrelated, but in addition to these I also gave other information to the querent, including how the project would affect his career and how he would proceed afterwards. (For an interpretation of this chart, see Figure 32 in Ch. 7 below.)

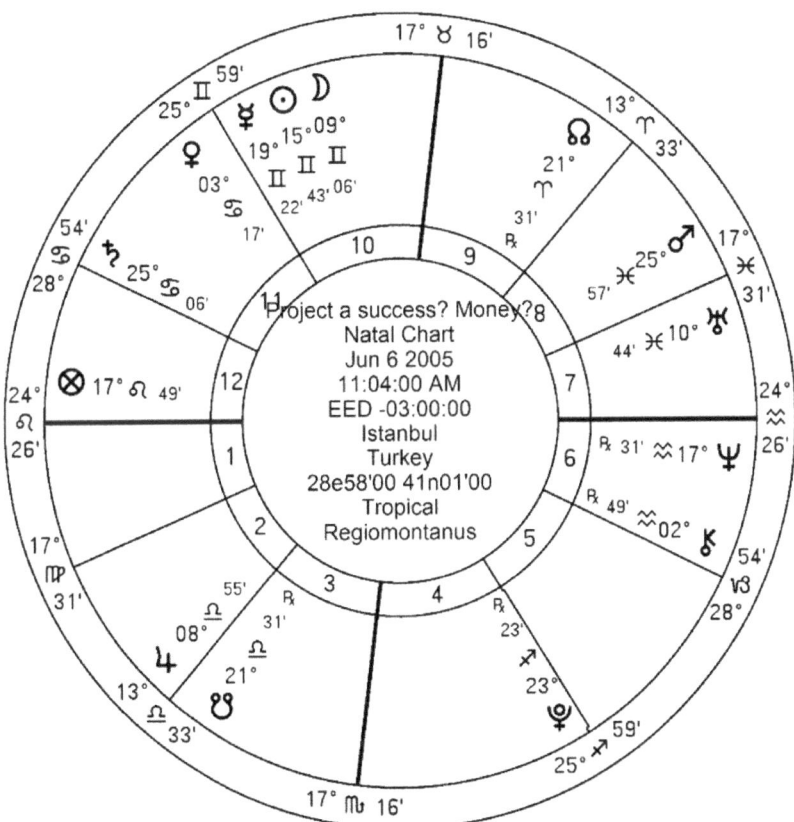

**Figure 11: Will this project be a success?
Will I get my money?**

2: SIGNIFICATORS

Before judgment, one of the most important things is to determine the significator and house which represent the querent and the quaesited. If you cannot determine the house and significators properly, you cannot make a correct judgment about the question.

Significators of the querent

Significators of the querent are the Ascendant, the lord(s) of the Ascendant, the lord of the intercepted sign in the 1st house (if any), and any planet in the 1st house. If there are more than one significator in the 1st house, the one which describes the querent better should be used. Questions asked from the first person as "we" are also related to the 1st house: for instance, the question "Shall we move to another house?" is also a 1st house question even though it involves multiple people.

The Moon is usually the co-significator of the querent; in order for her to also be the primary significator, Cancer should be rising. But if Cancer is the 7th house in a 7th house question, the Moon is instead related to the quaesited. In some cases, the Moon may also be the significator of the quaesited thing or person. But in my opinion the Moon represents the general course of events, which is indicated by the aspects which the Moon makes until she leaves her current sign. If the Moon is close to the cusp of any house, the house she applies to should be considered.

I use the planet which the Moon most recently aspected, in order to investigate the most recent dimensions of the event or the conditions the querent met with; the house ruled by that planet may likewise help us understand the most recent situation. The victor (also called the "almuten") of the Ascendant can be considered the primary significator of the querent, especially if it is stronger than the lord of the sign.

Māshā'allāh made some assessments about using the lord of the Ascendant or the Moon as the lord of the querent:[1]

- If the lord of the Ascendant looks at or aspects the Ascendant, the lord of the Ascendant should be the significator, as this planet is naturally more suited to be the significator.
- If the lord of the Ascendant does not aspect the Ascendant, then see if it applies to another planet which aspects the Ascendant.[2]
- If the lord of the Ascendant does not fulfil the above criteria, then take the Moon if she aspects the Ascendant or applies to a planet which does.
- If neither the lord of the Ascendant nor the Moon fulfils those criteria and if they are both void in course, prefer the one which is closer to the last degrees of its sign.
- See which planet the lord of the Ascendant or Moon will aspect first, once it has changed signs: if this first aspect is with a benefic, there is an opportunity for development because a void-in-course significator is not a good indicator for the development of the matter.
- Finally, whichever one of the two is the main significator (that is, the lord of the Ascendant or the Moon), the other one should still be used as a co-significator.

The lord of the Ascendant

With few exceptions, the lord of the Ascendant is always the primary significator of the querent, so the house it is in should be taken into consideration: that house indicates the current state and condition of the querent. Olivia Barclay notes that the house where the lord of the Ascendant is, indicates the place of the

---

[1] Māshā'allāh, *On Reception* Ch. 2 (pp. 444-47).
[2] **BD**: The reasoning here is that we want the lord's light to be carried back somehow to the rising sign, so as to produce a smoother result.

querent: if it is in the 6th house, the querent is at work; if in the 5th, he is having fun; if in the 4th, at home. If the lord of the Ascendant accompanies another planet, the querent is with someone else.[3] Additionally, the sign in which the lord of the Ascendant is, defines the querent.[4]

Separating aspects of the lord of the Ascendant indicate what the querent has done and experienced in the past; applying aspects indicate possible situations which the querent may meet with in the future. If the applying aspects are negative (and especially to malefics), the querent meets some difficulties and problems; if they are positive (and especially to benefics or strongly-placed planets), the querent meets positive developments and his chances for success are high.

As many astrologers agree, a burned or combust lord of the Ascendant shows that the astrologer is misinformed. According to Lilly, if the significator of the querent is burned, it indicates that the querent is in great fear or overpowered by some great person. If the lord of the Ascendant (which is the significator of the querent) is burned, the answer for this question will not be positive and the querent will be unhappy because of the astrologer's judgment. He adds: "If the Lord of the Ascendant be Combust, neither [the] question propounded will take, or the Querent be regulated."[5]

The Moon

The Moon indicates conditions which change quickly, indecision, instability, and a change of direction. As the Moon is a celestial body which moves fast and is reflective, it transfers the light between the other planets.[6] In this sense the Moon maintains

---

[3] Barclay, p. 131.
[4] Barclay, p. 131.
[5] Lilly, p. 123.
[6] **BD**: This is also called "translating" light.

communication between the people represented by the planets she connects with, and the connection between the matters and subjects ruled by them. The placement of the Moon by house and sign, and the Moon's aspects, help us understand how things will improve.

As mentioned above, in horary astrology the Moon is generally the co-significator of the querent and represents the desires and feelings of the querent at the moment of the question. The mind is where the Moon is. In some special cases, the Moon may be the significator of the quaesited (a person, object, or animal).

But Māshā'allāh's instructions about the differences between the Moon and the lord of the Ascendant did have an influence on contemporary astrologers. For instance, according to Olivia Barclay the lord of the Ascendant states the facts and where the querent is, whereas the Moon indicates personal interest. If the lord of the Ascendant is in the 6th house, the querent is currently "at work" or ill; but if the Moon is there, 6th house matters are on the querent's mind. The place of the Moon also indicates where one's hopes are. If the Moon is at the cusp of the 9th house in the question "Shall I go abroad?", the querent hopes to go abroad.[7]

Again, if the astrologer is asking the question, the Ascendant itself, the lord of the Ascendant, and the Moon represent the astrologer.[8]

Significators of the quaesited

From the beginning one must consider what or whom the question is really about, and look at the planets ruling the relevant house as well as planets in it. For questions about other people generically, the lords of the sign on the 7th and planets in the 7th are the significators of the quaesited. If there are many significators in

---

[7] Barclay, pp. 132-33.
[8] Barclay, p. 135.

the 7th house, the one which best describes the quaesited should be used as the significator.

Some astrologers argue that all questions relating to people who are specifically named, are found in the 7th house.[9] I do not agree with this opinion. Let's assume that I asked a question such as "Shall my sister, Ayşe, move to another house?" In March and McEvers's point of view, since I mentioned my sister's name all of the 7th house significators would indicate my sister. But from my point of view this is not logical. Siblings are represented by the 3rd house, planets in it, and its lord, even if they are denoted by their names.

If it is more powerful than the sign lord, the victor of the sign which is intercepted within the house representing the quaesited or matter, may be considered as the primary significator of the quaesited.

Olivia Barclay says, "The literal placement of the symbol often will tell you the literal placement of the person or thing asked about. If they are isolated planets, they are alone. If they are with another, the quesited is with another."[10]

The dignity or weakness of the quaesited's significator gives information about the quaesited's condition. If the significator is in its exaltation, the quaesited has good opinions regarding him. In other words, the chart features helps us to describe the characters involved.

According to Olivia Barclay, the placement of the significators in the chart is crucial. She says, "For example, if you ask if someone is at home and his significator is angular, then he is. (If the person does not mean anything in particular to you, take the seventh ruler as his indicator, but if he is an intimate friend take the eleventh house ruler.) If the significators are in succedent houses the per-

---

[9] March and McEvers, pp. 5, 12.
[10] Barclay, p. 132.

son is not far from home; if they are in cadent houses the person is far from home. If your significator perfects an aspect toward the symbol of the quesited, then you will meet each other."[11]

If the question is asked about another person, the house that symbolizes this person should be considered, including through derived houses. For instance, if a person asks a question about his spouse, the horary chart should be reviewed through the 7th house. But if you ask a question about your spouse's sibling, the 9th house should be considered (the 3rd from the 7th). If the question is about your mother's book, you should check the 11th house (the 2nd from the 10th). In the case of a specific object such as a book, Mercury would also be considered because he naturally indicates books.

The sign and the house where the significator is placed, shows where it is. For instance, in the case of a book if the significator is in Libra, the book is in the west. If the significator is in one of the angular houses, the book is somewhere in the house and very close to you.

Natural significators

Before judging a question, the natural significator of the question should be determined, because it sometimes helps in judgment more than the lord of the related house does. Additionally, natural significators also indicate whether or not the question is radical or not.

The natural significator is the planet which naturally indicates or rules the relevant topic or person through its very nature. For example, the Sun and Mars are natural significators of male figures, whereas the Moon and Venus are the natural significators for female figures. When making a judgment on the question "Shall I divorce my husband?" the relationship between the lords of the 1st

---

[11] Barclay, p. 133.

house and the Sun should be considered in addition to observing the lords of the 1st and the 7th.

Additional considerations

Some other points should be taken into consideration:

- The 4th house should be considered, to indicate the end of the matter.
- The 11th house is related to the querent's hopes and wishes. Positive aspects between the lord of the 11th and the lord of the Ascendant indicate the answer will be positive.
- Positive aspects between the significators, or positive aspects with the house cusps which are related to the question, also indicate that the answer will be positive.
- Previous aspects of the Moon indicate past experiences. All aspects which the Moon makes before exiting the sign she is in, show how the issues will develop and provide the opportunity to have a global view of future events. The final aspect of the Moon indicates how the issue ends. Also, from the most recent aspect of the Moon we may conclude what made the querent ask such a question. The coming aspects of the Moon indicate the steps during the course of the events and help to understand how the issue will end. (However, the judgment should not be only based on the final aspect of the Moon.)

Will the answer be positive or negative?

In answering this question, astrologers of the traditional period took into consideration any planet located in the 1st house. If supported by other factors, benefics (Jupiter, Venus, the North Node, and the Lot of Fortune) in the 1st indicate a positive answer for the question. They indicate that good things will occur. The North Node indicates that a lost item will be found, Venus that good things will happen, Jupiter brings luck and indicates that the querent will be protected. The Sun and the Moon may also be considered benefic.

A planet in the 1st house, especially if it is close to the degree of the Ascendant, indicates the querent's physical appearance, attitudes, talents, and advantages or disadvantages. For instance, if the Sun is rising it indicates that the question is something important and the querent will be dignified. The Moon rising indicates fluctuations, uncertainties, and insecurities. As the Moon indicates the public, the people may play some role in the conclusion of the issue. Mercury in the 1st indicates that the question is about some documents or short journeys. Other planets may also be considered in the same way. Lilly regularly used the following criteria for confirming the querent's physical features:

- The sign on the Ascendant, and its lord.
- The Moon and the sign she is in.
- Planets in the 1st house.
- Planets in aspect with the Ascendant and the Moon.

He also considered:
- The sign where the lord of the Ascendant is, the dispositors of the planets in the Ascendant, and their bound or term lords.

If supported by other elements of the chart, malefics in the 1st house bring a negative answer. These malefics are Saturn, Mars, and the South Node. Lilly once told a woman that she would not get pregnant, as the South Node was in the 1st house of the horary chart.[12]

Saturn in the 1st house, especially if he is retrograde, indicates a negative answer and the querent may have some evil experiences.

---

[12] Lilly, pp. 238-39.

According to Lilly, a retrograde Saturn in the 1st rarely brings a good end.[13] However, if the other factors are positive, then Saturn brings some damage but does not prevent the outcome. He brings restrictions and delays. Saturn in this house indicates that the issue will reach a critical point. The querent may feel anxious, depressed, frightened, and he may be ill.

Mars in the 1st house indicates difficulties and disputes for the querent. The querent needs to fight for, and/or make a lot of effort and show courage in order to obtain what he wants.

In terms of the modern, "outer" planets, some modern astrologers consider Uranus, Neptune, and Pluto to be malefics. Joan McEvers only considered Pluto as malefic; she states that the Moon, Mercury, Uranus, and Neptune may be either malefic and benefic. Uranus in the 1st house indicates an unpredictable and unexpected development of events. When Uranus is significant, conditions may change and separations may happen. Neptune indicates that the querent is confused and has lost touch with reality. Pluto indicates difficulties, extensive changes, and that the querent has less control over events.

If one of the Nodes is rising, it indicates the querent is experiencing some fated and unavoidable events. Planets on the same degree with the Nodes also indicate fated themes or crises. So, any planet on the Nodal degrees is important as it represents the fated dimension of events.

Lilly composed a table for examining and comparing the fortitudes and debilities of the planets, which gives them points in a horary chart.[14] If the benefics are strong, the answer of the question is possibly positive, while if the malefics are emphasized, negative things may be dominant. Lilly argues that the judgment should be delayed when benefics and malefics are equal. He states:

---

[13] Lilly, p. 122.
[14] Lilly, p. 115.

"When the testimonies of Fortunes and Infortunes are equal, defer judgment, it's not possible to know which way the Balance will turn: however, defer you your opinion till another question better inform you."[15]

Aspects

The aspects between significators in a horary chart have major importance. Conjunctions bring the querent and quaesited together physically or mentally, and maintain a close relationship between them. The strengths of planets in a conjunction will be united. Among these, conjunctions with the Sun, Venus, Jupiter, and also the Moon and Mercury, bring positive answers; those with Mars, Saturn, Pluto, and sometimes Uranus, bring negative results.

To generalize the opinions of both traditional and modern astrologers, we usually see an approach which assumes that squares and oppositions bring a "no" answer, whereas sextiles and trines mean "yes." If the Moon is transferring the light between the two significators, the answer is "yes"; if the Moon is in negative aspects with them, the answer is "no." Mutual reception between the significators strengthens the possibility of a positive answer.

I personally think that all of these assumptions vary depending on which planets are in aspect. For instance, inharmonious aspects between benefics may bring a positive result, but only after experiencing some difficulties. If there is a mutual reception between these significators, the potential of getting a positive answer becomes more likely. Harmonious aspects between malefics may bring unexpected negative outcomes, especially if these malefics are the lords of the 4th, 6th, 8th, or 12th houses. If they are in one of these houses and in harmonious aspects, the negative influences become apparent and negative results may occur.

---

[15] Lilly, p. 123.

As per commonly held rules, trines and sextiles indicate mutual harmony. If there is a trine between the main significators, there is cooperation and solidarity between the querent and the quaesited. Significators connected by a trine indicate a positive answer to the question. As compared with trines, sextiles require more effort, while trines bring good luck and success without too much effort.

Oppositions indicate that the querent and quaesited will move in different directions due to their disagreements. They bring arguments and disappointments. If the significator of the querent is applying by opposition to the significator of the quaesited, it means the querent is about to take action which the quaesited may disagree with. Olivia Barclay states that oppositions are "separative" aspects: the issue goes nowhere. But if there is a mutual reception between the significators in opposition, then some temporary results may be accomplished.[16] According to Sue Ward, planets in opposition bring conflicts even if they are well placed. Oppositions generally bring hostility, separations, and losses.[17]

Squares indicate that the querent and quaesited challenge or block each other's activities. They are considered negative and they indicate barriers that need to be overcome. They are energetic aspects which sometimes conclude the matter, but the querent feels upset. Squares indicate barriers, difficulties, losses, and the need for showing more effort. They represent stress and tension between the significators. Olivia Barclay states that squares resolve the issues through challenges. The houses involved in a square aspect, and the dignities of the planets in square, should be considered. If the planets are in their essential dignities, then a positive outcome may be expected even if it is by means of difficulties.[18]

---

[16] Barclay, p. 140.
[17] Ward, *Foundation*, Lesson 2, p. 19.
[18] Barclay, pp. 140-41.

A quincunx indicates that things have gone awry and they should be organized or regulated. There is a need for reconstruction or renegotiation in relation to the question. In short, the quincunx indicates that the conditions should change before the possible answer.

Semi-sextiles may indicate a positive outcome, but they are not high performance aspects; we may not expect a perfect outcome.

In any case, the dignities and weaknesses of the planets should be considered. Well-placed planets are advantageous in driving developments according to their nature. On the contrary, weakly-placed planets are inadequate for bringing a conclusion as they are like a person in a place where he is not comfortable. The same is true for peregrine planets. According to Lehman, peregrine planets do not perform well in a question or bring a conclusion to the matter, even if they are in exact aspect.[19] In questions about theft, Lilly considered whether there was a peregrine planet in the 7th house, then he looked at the other angular houses, and finally in the 2nd house. If there is a peregrine planet in one of these houses, he considered it the significator of the thief.[20]

When two planets are applying by aspect to each other mutually (that is, one is direct and the other retrograde), the strength of the aspect increases. If they are in a positive aspect, positive developments occur more quickly than expected or in a stronger way; if they are in a negative aspect, negative developments occur more quickly than expected, or in a stronger way. If this aspect is in angular houses, its outcome becomes more visible and happens faster.

---

[19] Lehman, p. 44.
[20] Lilly, pp. 330-31. **BD**: One reason for this is that a peregrine planet doesn't "belong" where it is, since it has no dignity or power there—just as a thief doesn't belong in someone else's house.

Phases of the Moon

Phases of the Moon may be used for judging questions. The Moon in an earlier degree than the Sun and being burned or combust, is considered a negative condition. For questions asked after the New Moon, positive answers may be expected. If the question is asked during the Full Moon, the issue is about to reach a culmination and things are about to come to the surface.

If the planet which is the lord of the Full Moon which most recently preceded the question, is in the house of the quaesited, or in one of the angular houses, the answer will be positive and what is asked will be achieved. A positive aspect between the Moon and the Sun, when the luminaries are not afflicted by malefic planets, indicates a successful outcome.

Besieging

A significator that is between the malefic planets without the intervening body or aspect of another planet is "besieged": the answer to the question will be negative. Uranus, Neptune, and Pluto are also considered malefic. On the contrary, being placed between Jupiter and Venus will have a positive influence on the outcome. This besieging by benefics is similar to "being in Heaven."

A planet in the same degree with the Nodes

In horary astrology, the North Node is considered benefic while the South Node is considered malefic. According to Sue Ward, the house in which the North Node is placed gets lucky and the house in which the South Node is placed becomes unlucky and helpless. For instance, the North Node in the 11th house indicates profit through friends, whereas the South Node in the same house indicates losses or scandals through friends.[21]

---

[21] Ward, *Foundation* Lesson 3, p. 11.

The North Node is one of the features which helps a positive outcome. It brings a private cooperation with the people related to the house it is in. Reinhold Ebertin states that the North Node is similar to an ally who maintains contact between people.[22] To put it simply, there is profit where the North Node is. On the other hand, the South Node brings damages, losses, and deprivation, in accordance with the topics of the house it is located in.

Retrogradation

If the significator of the querent is retrograde, the querent or the key person in that matter will back down. The person represented by the retrograde planet (especially Mercury) may be harmed or may be returning an old situation, reuniting with someone, or reviewing an issue. The person represented by a retrograde planet should try his chances again.

A retrograde significator is passive and a receiver, so it is open to being under other influences.

First, the house where this retrograde planet is should be considered, or we should look at the lord of the house where the retrograde planet is. For instance, Saturn retrograde in the 1st indicates unluckiness and a negative outcome. Or if the lord of the 7th is retrograde, the astrologer cannot satisfy the querent with his judgment. If the question is about relationships, a retrograde lord of the 7th house may indicate that the other party is unwilling to compromise and will even want to give up. If the lord of the 4th is retrograde in a question about real estate matters, we may expect dissatisfaction regarding the property. If the lord of the 6th or 10th is retrograde, the querent may go back to his previous job.

As per commonly-held rules, a retrograde significator indicates that delays will occur regarding the things asked. A stationary planet which is about to turn retrograde indicates unluckiness, de-

---

[22] Reinhold Ebertin, p. 69.

lays, deadlock, and damages: so it is not the time for new beginnings. A planet which is stationary before turning to its direct motion indicates success that may be reached slowly and after having to deal with some problems.

Mercury retrograde may have an influence on the judgment even if he is not a significator related to that question. For instance, the person in question may change his mind about the issue. Mercury retrograde indicates problems in communication, and misunderstandings.

Timing

Aspects and conjunctions between the planets, and with house cusps, should be considered for predicting the time when the matter will occur. To determine the time, the indicators listed below should be considered:

- The aspect between the significators of the querent and the quaesited.
- The aspect between the Moon and the significators.
- The distance between a significator and the nearest house cusp.
- The number of degrees needed for the Moon to change signs (especially when the Moon is in the last degrees of a sign).

There are two scales regarding timing: one of them is symbolic and the other is in real time. So, if there are 5° between two significators, this might indicate five units of time (symbolic, see below), but it might require the actual time necessary for one planet to conjoin with the other. Both methods are seen in ancient texts.

Angular Houses	Succedent Houses	Cadent Houses
Cardinal signs (day)	Cardinal signs (week)	Cardinal signs (month)
Mutable signs (week)	Mutable signs (month)	Mutable signs (year)
Fixed signs (month)	Fixed signs (year)	Fixed signs (unknown)

Figure 12: Time units for degrees between significators

Significators are often in different elements or qualities. For instance, one of the significators may be in a cardinal sign but in one of the cadent houses, whereas the other significator is in a fixed sign and in a succedent house. These give different units of time. The timing may then depend on the quality of the question: which of the two time frames is more reasonable?

(Determining the spatial direction in which something is, or takes place, is also not straightforward, and the significators may give mixed messages. As a general rule, the major significators should be considered, and one should consider their sign and house placements.)

If two significators conjoin or make an aspect in angular houses, then if they are fast, in their dignities, and are well placed, the event happens within a short time. If the significator of the querent is also the dispositor of the quaesited, this is an even better situation. If the significators are in contact in succedent houses, the event takes more time, while contacts in cadent houses indicate a longer time. Contacts in the signs where a planet feels comfortable in (such as its joy), are also positive indicators: Saturn in Aquarius, Jupiter in Sagittarius, Mars in Scorpio, Venus in Taurus, Mercury in Virgo, the Sun in Leo, and the Moon in Cancer.

Changing signs

A planet may be in the last degrees of a sign. This means that the things represented by this planet are about to reach a culmination, things will be completed, and a new phase is coming up. It is also important to note whether the planet entering another sign will be dignified and become stronger, or conversely not dignified, and lose its strength and weaken. Changing signs mean changing conditions.

If a planet changes sign before reaching a slower planet, the answer will not be positive. For instance, let the Moon be in 10° Aries, and Mercury in 29° Cancer. Since Mercury will enter Leo before the Moon makes her exact square with him, the expected outcome will not be realized, and will be blocked.

The dispositor effect

The lord of the sign where a planet is placed has an effect on that planet—especially the planets ruling the Moon and Mercury. In today's natal astrology, dispositors seem to have been forgotten, but in horary astrology dispositors are important. The dispositor of the significator indicates the power of that significator. Lilly explains the importance of dispositors while answering the question "Shall I be rich?" In the chart of this question, Scorpio is at the cusp of the 2nd house. So, the querent's wealth is related to the placement of Mars (who rules Scorpio). Mars is rising in the 1st house, in Libra. Although the position of Mars in Libra makes us think that the answer will be negative, since his dispositor Venus is in a powerful placement and in a fixed sign (indicating stability), Lilly gave a positive answer to this question.[23]

A dispositor's position is important for all of the planets placed in the sign it rules. Even if a planet is weak or in detriment, if its

---

[23] Lilly, pp. 177, 186.

dispositor is well placed and they have good aspects with each other, the weaker planet will be supported.

A dispositor indicates who influences whom, who is ruled by whom, and who is related to what. For instance, if your question is about your relationship, and the quaesited's significator is in a sign ruled by your own significator, this is good: your relationship goes well. (An example would be if the Ascendant is Gemini, ruled by Mercury, and the lord of the 7th is Jupiter, in Virgo: also ruled by Mercury.) If these significators are in mutual reception and in aspect, this is better, especially if they are well aspected. If there is a hard aspect between the significators but there is also mutual reception, the answer is still positive but there will be some difficulties in reaching this outcome.

The strengths of planets

If a planet is strong in a horary chart, it has power over the issues it represents. The strengths of the planets are generally known as essential and accidental dignities. Essential dignities include the five basic dignities (house or domicile, exaltation, triplicity, bound or term, and face or decan), and the accidental dignities are due to other factors, such as being in one of the angular or succedent houses (especially in the 11th and 5th houses), having a harmonious aspect with one of the benefics, being fast, being ruled by a strong dispositor, or being in a house it is analogous to (such as the Sun being in the 10th, since both the Sun and the 10th pertain to fame and reputation).

Planets in angular houses are in their strongest positions. The more a planet is distant from the angles, the more its potential decreases; it seems alienated from its familiar environment. That's why the cadent houses are related to foreign and distant places and conditions. Being away from familiar places is defined as a malefic condition, because everyone is strong in his own place.

Planets in angular houses bring quick results, and planets in succedent houses bring slow results. However, on the other hand planets in cadent houses are so ineffective that they do not bring a result, or they bring it too late. For instance, if the question is about a missing person and there are good aspects involving planets in the angular houses, good news will arrive quickly and the querent will meet the missing person. If the planets are in angular houses and in detriment with hard aspects, then again news arrives quickly, but it may be bad news. If the significators are in cadent houses, there will be delays in the news or nothing will be heard about the matter.

	Angular	Succedent	Cadent
Strength	Strong	Medium	Weak
Finding lost item or missing person	Within the house or somewhere close to the querent	A little far away but not too much	Far away
Possibility	Strong	Medium	Too little
Timing of events	Fast (days)	Not soon (weeks)	Slow (months)
Prices	Good price	Fair price	Low price
Health, illness, death	Strong vitality, surviving the risk of death	Changeable, may be good or bad	Poor vitality, illness, or death

Figure 13: Time units for degrees between significators

In a question about a lost item, if the significators are in angular houses the lost item will be found. However, if the significators are in cadent houses the item may not be found.

As the planets in angular houses are strong, the person and the issues they represent are also strong and remarkable. If such a planet represents a person, the person is strong enough to overcome all difficulties. If the planet represents an illness, then it is a malicious one. Therefore, the lord of the 6th house in one of the cadent houses is a good indicator for questions about health.

Fixed stars

In *Christian Astrology*, William Lilly used approximately 40 fixed stars, although he did not appear to use them much. However, I do use many fixed stars in addition to the significators, and I advise my students to use fixed stars in horary judgments. Note: it is the conjunctions of the fixed stars that are crucial (not aspects), using a maximum orb of 1.5° - 2°.

Lots

Lots (in the past, sometimes called "Arabic Parts") are used in both horary and natal astrology. For instance, when answering the question "Shall I marry Ali?" the Lot of marriage may be used. Or, the Lot of death may be used for a question such as "Is he alive?"

The Lot of Fortune, which is one of the most important Lots, is a significator of prosperity and luck, and it is often used in natal astrology. It helps us determine in which parts of life the native will be lucky and from which fields of life he will make profit. Even if the question is not related to money and prosperity, I believe that the position of the Lot should be considered because it may show us where and how the greatest luck and possibilities for the querent are found, and to whom or what they are related.

It is better to consider the Lot of Fortune along with the position of its lord. If its lord is well placed and in a strong position, and in aspect with the luminaries, the querent may have good luck and opportunities. The planet which makes an aspect to the Lot of Fortune indicates the fields of life or subjects from which profit and opportunities will stem.

Vettius Valens, al-Bīrūnī, Manilius, Firmicus Maternus, and many others calculated the Lot of Fortune differently by day and night. By day they calculated from the Sun forward in the zodiac to the Moon, and then projected this distance from the Ascendant (this is also expressed as Moon − Sun + Ascendant). By night, they calculated from the Moon forward to the Sun, and projected from the Ascendant (also expressed as Sun − Moon + Ascendant). Ptolemy used the day formula all of the time, just as Lilly did, but it is important to change the formula by night, and I follow this. One reason is that the Sun is the diurnal luminary, and the Moon is the nocturnal luminary: so we should start from the luminary which actually rules the time of the chart (as Bonatti explains).[24]

House cusps

The Regiomontanus house system is mainly used in horary charts because house cusps are important and this system calculates the house cusps in a way which works best.

Lilly takes advantage of the house cusps in timing. For instance, in a question related to a soldier going abroad, he predicted the soldier would leave his home and go abroad 2 months later, as his significator was 2° away from the cusp of the 9th house. This is an example of the symbolic timing I mentioned above.

The planet which is on the cusp of a house has influence on the matters of that house.

Planets as significators

In horary astrology it is important to know what the planets represent by their natures. Below you will find some information about the things and people indicated by the planets.

Sun: Authorities, public officials, the life force, health, success, male figures (especially between ages 35-45), prominent people, superiors, employers, managers, illumination, power, ego, reliable people.

---

[24] Bonatti, Tr. VIII.2, Ch. 2 (p. 1043).

Moon: Mother (esp. in nocturnal charts), women in general, the public, temperament, fluctuations, emotions, changes, liquids, leakages, short journeys, moving house, lost items, things related to the sea.

Mercury: Writing, communication, transportation, books, letters, messages, questions, trade, contracts, negotiation, journeys, mental activities, young people, students, office workers, secretaries, salespeople, tradesmen, tricksters.

Venus: Love, gifts, harmony, alliances, relationships, marriage, social events, young women, the mother (in diurnal charts), wife, tastes, arts, luxurious items.

Mars: Sex, wars, seductiveness, energy, restlessness, fights, butchers, surgeons, incisions, assertiveness, leadership, weapons, fire, iron, accidents, danger, injuries, male figures between ages 25-35.

Jupiter: Expansion and growth, good luck, higher education, prosperity, long journeys, prediction, gamblers, success, professionals, wealthy people, lawyers, judges, horses, foreigners, middle-aged male figures.

Saturn: Barriers, limitations, losses, seriousness, toughness, delays, old things, old people, debts, poverty, real estate, construction, time, lethargy, distress, karma, death, loneliness, isolated people, the father (in nocturnal charts).

Uranus: Fractures, accidents, separation, surprises, awakening, electricity, New Age, coups, strikes; according to Barbara Watters, what is sudden, unexpected, and unpredictable.[25]

Neptune: Separation, confusion, abstraction, spirituality, fogginess, drugs, alcohol, deception, poetry, illusion, unreality, mysticism.

Pluto: Power, sexuality, something in-depth, underground, rebirth, transformation, transition, the subconscious, death.

---

[25] Watters, pp. 54-55.

Lot of Fortune: Money, income, possessions, lost items, good luck, treasure.

Benefics and malefics

In traditional astrology Mars, Saturn, and the South Node are defined as malefics, whereas Venus, Jupiter, the North Node, and the Lot of Fortune are defined as benefics. Contemporary astrologers tend to define Uranus, Neptune, and Pluto as malefics. On the other hand, some astrologers define Mars, Saturn, and Pluto as malefics, with Venus, Jupiter, and the Sun being benefics, and treat Mercury, Uranus, and Neptune, in accordance with their aspects and the question asked.[26]

When making a judgment about a horary chart, if the primary significators apply by harmonious aspects to the benefics we may expect positive developments on the matter; but if they apply to the malefics (especially with inharmonious aspects), they represent a negative outcome.

---

[26] March and McEvers, p. 15.

3: MEANINGS OF HOUSES IN GENERAL, AND IN HORARY ASTROLOGY

FIRST HOUSE

General meaning: Life, spirit, the form and shape of the body, physical appearance, first impressions, health and vitality, metabolism, the self, personality, those close to the native; the talents, creativity, speech, mental abilities, and humor of the native; all mental faculties, welfare, and happiness, the life force of the native, the emotional life, motivations, actions, desires, and wishes, character and profession of the native. As the degree of the Ascendant represents the beginning of life, this house is related to all types of beginnings.

In horary astrology: The querent's life, body, skin color, and form. In addition to the lord of the Ascendant, the condition of the 1st house and planets in it also indicate the querent's conditions. We may also identify the persons and issues with which the querent sympathizes and associates (like the football team he supports, the politician he votes for, or the artist he likes). As the 1st house represents the querent and the 7th house the quaesited (in a general way), the functioning and strengths of these houses also indicate the advantages and the disadvantages of the querent and quaesited relative to each other. For instance, if the lord of the 1st is stronger than the lord of the 7th, the querent has a higher status and power as compared to the quaesited.

SECOND HOUSE

General meaning: Monetary gains, incomes, investments, savings, expenditure, financial conditions, the native's luck in financial matters, his life experiences with finances, the livelihood, money lent, profit and loss, the native's assistants or supportive friends, his own financial resources (which are not dependent on others).

In horary astrology: Wealth, richness or poorness, goods and chattels, money lent, the querent's friends or assistants in court cases, the prosecutor's assistant in private matters. This house and the planets placed in it represent the querent's wealth and finances. This may be a car or stocks. The differences in the strengths of the lord of the 2nd and the lord of the 8th are important in questions regarding monetary issues. The lord of the 8th being stronger than the lord of the 2nd indicates that the querent loses money and his opponent makes profit.

THIRD HOUSE

General meaning: Siblings, neighbors, young relatives and relations with these people, acquaintances through marriage, short journeys, domestic journeys, education, reading, opinions, expressing opinions, information, researches, news, messengers, correspondences and letters, reports and messages, gossip.

In horary astrology: Siblings, cousins, neighbors, moving from one place to another; the shoulders, legs, hands, fingers. Messages, talk, gossip. A weak 3rd house indicates problems in written agreements. As this house is related to communication and gossip, malefic planets in this house indicate bad gossip and problems in communication.

FOURTH HOUSE

General meaning: Family, family's status, home or residence, home life, blood-relatives, father, ancestry, elder relatives, the past, roots, inheritances, ownership, real estate, the quality and nature of the land one purchases, the partner's or spouse's profession, the end of all matters or life, death, cemeteries, real estate, the family background of the native, hidden or buried treasures, hidden wealth.

In horary astrology: The querent's father, the condition of the properties that will be sold or purchased, the benefits or disadvantages of a house which is sought for the querent, buildings and gardens, borders, lost items and missing people, hidden things, the end of matter that is asked. Fathers, soil, houses, real estate, inheritances, farms, buried treasures, ancient settlements, flower gardens, fields, crops.

FIFTH HOUSE

General meaning: Children, games, fun activities, entertainment venues, hobbies, collections, self-expression, arts, love and romanticism, sensual pleasures, feasts, sport activities, risks, speculations, medium distance journeys, apparel, agents, messengers and guides, ambassadors and legates, the wealth of the father.

In horary astrology: The querent's children, questions about pregnancy, determining the gender of unborn offspring; the querent's father's or family's financial situation and the values they have, questions about things to be inherited from the father, all types of entertainment activities. Children in general, messengers, the condition of a pregnant woman, feasts, pubs, games.

SIXTH HOUSE

General meaning: Excessive and detailed works, projects that need to be focused on deeply, subordinates and servants of the native, craftsmen, tenants (of both land and rental properties), stress, illnesses and weaknesses, the quality of and reason for the illnesses; pets, questions concerning small cattle or animals, responsibilities and duties, abilities gained through practice, lower social status, forced labor, uncles and aunts.[77]

In horary astrology: The querent's illnesses and weaknesses, subordinates and employees, tenants, pets and cattle, working for others, forced labor. The quality of and reason for the querent's illness, if it is curable or not, if it will last long or not. Farmers, uncles and aunts.

SEVENTH HOUSE

General meaning: Partnership, marriage, open enemies, challenges, discussions and oppositions, contests, rivalry, the physical existence of partners and spouse, contracts and agreements, consulting, court cases, the public, the social life of the native, death, alternative living places.

In horary astrology: Fugitives or perpetrators, open enemies and competitors, consultants, the place to which one considers moving. The quality of the marriage, the characteristics of the proposed partner or spouse, all questions concerning love matters; open enemies, the defendant in a court case, the enemy in wars, all types of discussions and fights, thieves and thefts, the spouse's or partner's physical appearance. In horary charts, the 7th also indicates the astrologer who receives the question. If the 7th house is afflicted, the astrologer may have some troubles or be incapable of answering the question. If the question is concerning relationships, then the 7th is considered specifically for that (and not for the astrologer). The same house is considered in questions relating to court cases and competitors.

---

[77] **BD**: Döşer says this because the sixth is the third (siblings) from the fourth (parents).

EIGHTH HOUSE

General meaning: Death, wills, inheritances, fears, difficulties, dangers, surgical operations (due to the risk of death), profit coming from partnerships and other people, the finances of the partner or spouse, shared resources, opportunities coming from or depending on others, taxes, expenditures, the assistants and supporters of the competitors, the friends of the defendant in court cases.

In horary astrology: Issues related to debts and loans. Death, inheritances, and shared resources. According to Deborah Houlding, if the querent seeks to borrow money but the lord of the 8th is stronger than the lord of the 2nd, the lender (the 8th) is in a better position than the borrower (the 2nd).[78] For questions related to the finances of the partner or spouse, inheritances, and dangerous situations, the 8th house should be considered.

NINTH HOUSE

General meaning: Religious matters and people, religious journeys, spiritual issues, books and studies, learning and teaching, giving lectures, higher education, long distance journeys, scientific issues, foreign countries, connections with foreign people and countries, foreign trade, exports, astrology, astrologers and theologians, dreams, publishing, researches, legal issues, laws, courts, advanced talents, wisdom, the search for truth, consulting in spiritual issues, expanding higher consciousness, one's life-perspective, the relatives of the spouse, the second spouse.

In horary astrology: Overseas travel and long journeys, religious people, dreams, books and learning, the relatives of the spouse. Grandchildren, foreign lands and people, foreign trade and

---

[78] Houlding, p. 80.

the success of journeys. Religious issues, clergymen, lawyers. Predictions and astrology are also related to the 9th house.

TENTH HOUSE

General meaning: Professions and occupations, the realization of goals, efforts in the 1st house realized in the outer world, communication with the outer world, fate and destiny, fortune, managers, bosses, royal or strong people, the status of the native, goals for the future, the judgment in court cases, judges, the native's actions, social status, and reputation, career, managerial positions, professional abilities, stability in the career, success, rewards, talents, the mother.

In horary astrology: The querent's profession or daily occupations, status, career and business life. People in authority in relation to the querent himself, or leaders in general.

ELEVENTH HOUSE

General meaning: Friends and friendship, the loyalty or disloyalty of friends, groups, the social life of the native or those with whom the native socializes, politics, unexpected good luck and achievements, hopes and wishes, confidence, compliments, and critics. It indicates happiness. As a planet in this house reaches the 10th house in primary motion, it is called the house of hopes and wishes. Being the second house from the 10th, it indicates those who help the native, and his finances in professional endeavors. (Succedent houses are always supportive houses.)

In horary astrology: The querent's friends, stepchildren, income earned from professional endeavors and efforts, his mother's or boss's finances (according to the question that is asked). If the querent has a secret wish which he does not want to reveal, the 11th house indicates if the querent's wish may come true or not.

Significators in this house are considered positive indicators, as this is the house of hopes, support, good luck, comfort, and welfare.

TWELFTH HOUSE

General meaning: Hidden enemies, jealousies, behind-the-scenes activities or gossip, slander, suffering, problems and difficulties, sorrows, dangers, losses, misfortunes, tricks, secluded or isolated places, hospitals, prisons, prisoners, exiles, secret love affairs, secrets, being unaware of other people, self-undoing, self-destruction, karmic debts, worries, secrets, witches, dealing with magic, mistakes, deceptions.

In horary astrology: Hidden enemies, people dealing with magic, those in prison, larger cattle and animals, diseases and losses, working hard but gaining little, private affairs.

4: SIGNS, COUNTRIES, REGIONS, CITIES, & PLACES

Ancient astrologers were often asked questions about the location of a missing item or lost person. When answering questions about lost ships, missing people, slaves, lost animals, and objects, astrologer William Lilly determined the direction of such lost things through the signs where the significators were placed, and both the element and the quality of the significator, and the areas this significator ruled, helped the astrologer make a judgment.

We know Lilly lived in an era of overseas discoveries and new trading opportunities long before the invention of reliable longitude measurement tools. Overseas travel was extremely dangerous and fraught with many difficulties: as a consequence, many people asked about the location of ships at sea that were missing or late, and the fate of their crews. There was a huge demand for horary astrology in port cities, and questions about the safety of any ship were typical. Lilly even tried to determine which parts of that ship were damaged when he received a question about a missing ship. He prepared a list showing the link between the signs and the parts of ship: if a sign's lord was in detriment, the corresponding part of the ship is damaged.

In Lilly's scheme,[79] Aries indicated the "breast"[80] of the ship; Taurus, under the breast a little towards the water; Gemini: the rudder or stern; Cancer, the bottom or floor of the ship; Leo, the top of the ship above water; Virgo, the belly of the ship; Libra, what is sometimes above or below the water, or "between wind

---

[79] Lilly, p. 158. **BD**: This is based on the scheme as reported in al-Rijāl, *The Book of the Skilled* Ch. II.14 (first part); see also the Latin version of ʿUmar al-Tabarī in *Judges* §9.41.

[80] **BD**: In the Latin version of al-Tabarī, the prow.

and weather";[81] Scorpio, where the seamen are lodged or perform their offices;[82] Sagittarius, the mariners themselves;[83] Capricorn, the ends of the ship;[84] Aquarius, the captain;[85] Pisces, the oars.

Lee Lehman translates these identifications into the parts of a car for questions about buying and selling a car: Aries, the front end of the car; Taurus, the passenger compartment; Gemini, the steering mechanism, column, and wheel; Cancer, the floor or underside and oil pan; Leo, the roof, sun roof, antennas, and convertible top; Virgo, the trunk or storage area; Libra, the paint job and aerodynamics; Scorpio, the motor; Sagittarius, the passengers; Capricorn, the bumpers and crash protectors; Aquarius, the driver; Pisces, the wheels and axles.[86]

Countries, regions and cities ruled by the signs are considered in mundane astrology. There are many ways to do this, but for each method, the signs where we find significators and their aspects will indicate events in the countries and regions ruled by those signs. The following lists of countries are primarily based on Claudius Ptolemy, al-Qabīsī,[87] Lilly, H.S. Green, and Ivy M. Goldstein-Jacobson.

ARIES

The ancient astrologers associated Aries with sandy and hilly grounds and barren places. According to William Lilly, Aries placed

---

[81] **BD**: In the Latin version of al-Rijāl, what is "raised up" and "pressed down" or lowered, of the breast of the ship. Meaning uncertain.
[82] **BD**: In the Latin version of al-Tabarī, the place of the mast.
[83] **BD**: In the Latin version of al-Tabarī, the mast.
[84] **BD**: In the Latin version of al-Tabarī, the ropes, sail, and yard-arm.
[85] **BD**: In the Latin version of al-Tabarī, the sailors.
[86] Lehman, p. 58.
[87] **BD**: I have updated this list based on the Arabic; in the first edition, Döşer's list was taken from Bonatti's version, which was rather garbled. Almost all of the Arabic place names refer to parts of the old Sasanian Persian or Muslim Abbasid empires.

at the cusp of the 4th in horary charts about buying lands, indicates that the land is hilly and full of hard rocks. Places ruled by Aries are of a Martian nature. Places which are hot or close to heat, where effort is made, places where there is aggression and violence, where blood is shed, are of the nature of Aries. Al-Bīrūnī also related Aries to places where jewelry is produced.[88]

Direction: East.

Places: Where sheep and cattle feed or used to be, sandy and hilly grounds, a place of refuge for thieves; in houses, the covering, ceiling, or plastering of it, the stable of small beasts, lands newly taken in or newly ploughed, or where bricks have been burned, or lime has been used or made.[89] Places where repair tools and tools for special purposes are stored or used, places close to heat, places where glass is made, furnaces, places related to things with blood, places where aggression is seen. Places where jewelry is produced.

Countries, Regions, and Cities: *Al-Qabīsī:*[90] Babylonia, Persian, Azerbaijan, Palestine. *Lilly:*[91] Germany, Swabia, Poland, Burgundy, France, England, Denmark, Upper Silesia, Judea, Syria; Florence, Capua, Naples, Ferrara, Verona, Utrecht, Marseilles, Augusta, Caesarea, Padua, Bergamo. *H. S. Green:* Burgundy, England, Denmark, Germany, Palestine, Lower Poland, Syria, Birmingham, Blackburn, Oldham, Leicester, Brunswick, Capua, Cracow, Florence, Marseilles, Nepal, Padua, Saragossa, Verona. *Ivy Goldstein-Jacobson* adds: Galicia, United Kingdom, Israel, Lebanon.

---

[88] Al-Bīrūnī, §366.
[89] Lilly, p. 93.
[90] **BD**: The lists of al-Qabīsī are from his *Introduction* Ch. I.25 – I.36.
[91] **BD**: The lists of Lilly are from pp. 93-99.

TAURUS

The ancient astrologers associated Taurus with places where food is stored and the stables of large animals like buffalos and elephants. Places ruled by Taurus are of the nature of Venus. Venus represents precious things and jewelry. Considering also that the Moon is exalted in Taurus, we may understand why ancient astrologers associated Taurus with places of food and beverages, where they are stored, and fertile lands. As Taurus is the second sign, modern astrologers connect Taurus with the 2nd house and monetary issues. As a result, banks and money-boxes are related to Taurus. According to Lilly, Taurus placed at the cusp of the 4th house in horary charts about buying lands means the land is flat and ideal for shepherds, feeding animals, or cultivation.

Direction: South-southeast.

Places: Stables where horses are, low houses, houses where the implements of cattle are stored, pasture or feeding grounds where no houses are; near plain grounds, or where bushes have been recently dug up and where wheat and corn is sown, some little trees not far off; in houses, cellars and low rooms. Banks, money-boxes, jewelry boxes, places where wheat and corn are stored. Places where leather goods such as shoes are stored. Places where food is stored, like the cellar or refrigerator.

Countries, Regions, and Cities: *Al-Qabīsī:* the Sawād,[92] Māhān, Hamadhān, the country of the Kurds. *Lilly:* Greater Poland, northern Sweden,[93] Russia, Ireland, Switzerland, Lorraine, Campania, Persia, Cyprus, Parthia, Novrogod, Parma, Bologna, Palermo, Mantua, Sienna, Brescia, Karlstad, Nantes, Leipzig, Herbipolis. *H.S. Green:* Asia Minor, Caucasus, Cyprus, Georgia, Grecian Archipelago, Ireland, Iran, Poland, Belarus ("White Russia"), Ashton-under-Lyne, Dublin, Leipzig, Mantua, Parma,

---

[92] **BD**: This is the fertile region of black soil around the fertile crescent, Syria, and Iraq.
[93] **BD**: *Sweathland*, an older English designation.

Palermo, Rhodes, St. Louis. *Ivy Goldstein-Jacobson* adds: Northern Anatolia, Egypt, Holland, Odessa.

GEMINI

The ancient astrologers associated Gemini with airy, windy, and high places, as Gemini is an airy sign. Its lord Mercury is related to airy places and a windy atmosphere. Places ruled by Gemini are Mercurial in nature: that is, places related to knowledge and communication. Books and documents are also of the nature of Mercury. Naturally, where these things are kept is also attributed to Gemini. As Mercury and Gemini, which is the third sign of the zodiac, are connected to travel, modern astrologers relate Gemini with transportation vehicles. According to Lilly, if Gemini is placed at the cusp of the 4th house in a horary chart in a question about buying land, the place is neither hilly nor flat, some of it is good and some not that good.

Direction: West-southwest.

Places: An office, library, cars, trains, buses, places where documents and files are kept, desks, places of education, schools, and bookstores. High places, the highest place of a room, airy places, telephones, phone lines, cabinets, thermometers, and measurement tools. Hills, high places, and places where mental work is done are also ruled by Gemini. According to al-Bīrūnī, places related to acrobats, musicians, and also palaces are ruled by Gemini.[94]

Countries, Regions, and Cities: *Al-Qabīsī*: Jurjān, Greater Armenia, Azerbaijan, al-Jīlān, Mūqān, Egypt, Barqa. *Lilly*: Lombardy, Brabant, Flanders, the West and Southwest of England, Armenia, London, Louvain, Bruges, Nuremberg, Cordova, Hasford, Mont, Bamberg, Cesena. *H. S. Green*: Northeast shores of Africa, Armenia, Belgium, Brabant, Lower Egypt, Flanders, Lombardy,

---

[94] Al-Bīrūnī, §366.

Sardinia, Tripoli, United States of America, Wales, and West of England. *Ivy Goldstein-Jacobson* adds: Los Angeles, Plymouth, Uruguay, Versailles.

CANCER

The ancient astrologers associated Cancer with seas and places near water, as Cancer is a watery sign and its lord the Moon is associated with waters and the sea. Places ruled by Cancer are of the nature of the Moon. As the Moon indicates water, places in the home which are related to water such as laundry areas, or places connected to child care, nurses, and nursing, come under the Moon. According to Lilly, if Cancer is placed at the cusp of the 4th house in a horary chart for a question about buying land, this place is undoubtedly near water; there must be a river or lake near it.

Direction: North.

Places: Oceans, seas, great rivers, navigational waters; but in the inland countries it notes places near rivers, brooks, springs, wells, cellars in houses, wash-houses, marshy grounds, ditches with rushes, sedges, sea banks, trenches, cisterns. Damp places, the sink, kitchen, womb, tombs, graves, low places of rooms, places related to mothers and feeding, childcare rooms, nurseries. Additionally, it indicates places of worship according to al-Bīrūnī.[95]

Countries, Regions, and Cities: *Al-Qabīsī:* Lesser Armenia, Eastern Khurāsān, China, part of the country of Balkh and Azerbaijan. *Lilly:* Scotland, Zealand (in Denmark), Holland, Prussia, Tunisia, Algeria, Constantinople, Venice, Milan, Genoa, Amsterdam, York, Magdeburg, Wittenberg, Saint Lucas, Cadiz. *H. S. Green:* North and West Africa, Holland, Mauritius, Paraguay, Scotland, New Zealand, St. Andrews, Deptford, Manchester, Rochdale, York, New York, Algiers, Amsterdam, Bern, Cadiz, Istanbul (Con-

---

[95] Al-Bīrūnī, §366.

stantinople), Genoa, Lübeck, Magdeburg, Milan, Stockholm, Tunis, Venice. *Ivy M. Goldstein-Jacobson* adds: Anatolia.

LEO

The ancient astrologers associated Leo with the forests and wild animals as Leo represents the lion, the king of the forest and a wild animal. Being a fiery sign, Leo is related to hot and fiery places. Places ruled by Leo are of the nature of the Sun: hot, fiery, where nobles and notable people are, where children and young people are. Entertainment and fun places are ruled by Leo. Leo, ruled by the Sun, is related to acting, theaters, and nobles. Modern astrologers also connect Leo with the 5th house as it is the fifth sign, and so with children and playrooms. Like the other fiery signs, Leo represents places which are hilly and sandy, not suitable for agriculture. According to Lilly, if Leo is placed at the cusp of the 4th house in a horary chart for a question about buying land, it is hilly and sandy.

Direction: East-northeast.

Places: A place where wild beasts frequent, woods, forests, deserts, steep rocky places, inaccessible places, kings' palaces, castles, forts, parks; in houses, where fire is kept, near a chimney. Gardens, places of entertainment, playgrounds, theatres, kids' rooms, places related to creative activities, high and visible places. Fiery places and places near heat, remarkable places, places where nobles and titled people live.

Countries, Regions, and Cities: *Al-Qabīsī:* The land of the Turks to the ends of the inhabited world. *Lilly:* Italy, Bohemia, the Alps, Turkey, Sicily, Apulia, Rome, Syracuse, Cremona, Ravenna, Damascus, Prague, Linz, Koblenz, Bristol. *H. S. Green:* The Alps, Apulia, Bohemia, Chaldea, France, Italy, ancient Phoenicia around Tyre and Sidon, North Romania, Sicily, Bath, Blackpool, Bristol, Portsmouth, Taunton, Chicago, Philadelphia, Bombay, Damascus,

Prague, Ravenna, Rome. I*vy M. Goldstein-Jacobson* adds: Chicago, Lancashire.

VIRGO

The ancient astrologers associate Virgo with agriculture, so it is related to places where grains are found or stored. According to Lilly, if Virgo is placed at the cusp of the 4th house in a question about land, then the place is plain, ideal for shepherds, or an ideal field for herding and cultivating. Virgo also represents places of the nature of Mercury, its lord: so it is related to offices and libraries. Being the sixth sign of the zodiac, Virgo is attributed to the sixth house by modern astrologers, so places where illnesses and weaknesses are cured are ruled by this sign. Subordinates, employees, and the work environment are related to the sixth house.

Direction: South-southwest.

Places: It signifies a study where books are, a closet, dairy-house, cornfields, granaries, malt-houses, haystacks, stores of barley, wheat, or peas, or a place where cheese and butter is preserved and stored. Containers, the refrigerator, medicine cabinet, writing desk, offices, and physicians' offices.

Countries, Regions, and Cities: *Al-Qabīsī:* Jarāmaqa, Syria, the Euphrates, al-Jazīrah,[96] Persia. *Lilly:* Southern Greece, Croatia, the area of Athens, Mesopotamia, Africa, southwest France, Paris, Jerusalem, Rhodes, Lyons, Toulouse, Basel, Heidelberg, Brindisi. *H.S. Green:* Assyria, Babylon, Brazil, Crete, Turkey, Thessaly, Croatia, Greece, the Peloponnesian peninsula, Mesopotamia from the Tigris to the Euphrates, Silesia, Switzerland, Virginia, the West Indies, Bury, Cheltenham, Maidstone, Norwich, Reading, Todmorden, Boston (USA), Brindisi, Corinth, Heidelberg, Jerusalem,

---

[96] **BD**: Lit., "island." This is a flexible term, which can even refer to deserts surrounded by other landscapes. One of the Latin versions clarifies that this is Spain.

Lyons, Los Angeles, Paris, Padua, Strasburg, Toulouse. *Ivy M. Goldstein-Jacobson* adds: Baghdad, Navarre, the Caribbean, Yugoslavia, Zurich.

LIBRA

As it is an Air sign, ancient astrologers associated Libra with the outdoors and high grounds. Being ruled by Venus, Libra is also associated with smooth surfaces. According to Lilly, if Libra is placed at the cusp of the 4th house in a horary chart for a question about buying land, the place is neither hilly nor flat, some of it is good and some not that good. Libra, which represents one-on-one relations, sales, and marketing, is associated with the hawker's trade. It is also associated with bedrooms (being a sign of marriage and relationships). As it is ruled by Venus, Libra also indicates jewelry cases and wardrobes.

Direction: West.

Places: In fields it represents grounds near windmills, or a barn or outhouse, sawpits, or where barrel-makers work or wood is cut, the sides of hills, tops of mountains, grounds where hawking and hunting is practiced, sandy and gravelly fields, pure, clear, and sharp air, the upper rooms in houses, chambers, garrets, one chamber within another. According to al-Bīrūnī, it indicates mosques, places of worship, castles, observatories, and orchards.[97]

Countries, Regions, and Cities: *Al-Qabīsī:* The Byzantine empire and what borders on it up to Ifrīqīyyah, Upper Egypt up to the boundaries of Ethiopia and the boundaries of Barqa, Kirmān, Sijistān, Kabul, Tabaristān, Balkh, Hirāt. *Lilly:* Upper Austria, the dukedom of Savoy, Alsace, Livonia, Lisbon, Frankfurt, Vienna, Placentia, the Theban area of Greece, Arles, Fribourg, Spires. *H. S. Green:* Austria, Argentina, Burma, Caspian boundaries, China (es-

---

[97] Al-Bīrūnī, §366.

pecially in the north), regions of India near China, Upper Egypt, Japan, Livonia, Tibet, Savoy, Leeds, Middleton, Nottingham, Antwerp, Charleston, Copenhagen, Frankfurt, Fribourg, Gaeta, Jo-Johannesburg, Lisbon, Placenza, Spires, Vienna. *Ivy M. Goldstein-Jacobson* adds: Africa, Hawaii, Korea, the Pacific Ocean, Thailand, parts of South Africa ("Zululand").

SCORPIO

The ancient astrologers associate Scorpio with muddy waters, swamps, stinky waters, insects, and poisonous animals. According to Lilly, if Scorpio is placed at the cusp of the 4th house in a horary chart for a question about buying land, the place is undoubtedly near water; there must be a river or lake nearby. Lilly states that Scorpio should not be at the cusp of the 4th house when the querent moves to another house, because it indicates there will be some problems with insects and the sewer system. As Mars rules Scorpio, Scorpio is associated with prisons, places where blood is shed, butchers, and surgeries. Scorpio also represents death, so it indicates places of mourning. As Scorpio is one of the mute signs, it also indicates desolate and silent places. As Scorpio indicates the urinary system, it is associated with toilets, water outlets, and sinks.

Direction: North-northeast.

Places: Places which all sorts of creeping beasts use, such as beetles or those which lack wings and are poisonous; gardens, orchards, vineyards, the ruins of houses near waters; muddy, moorish grounds, stinking lakes, quagmires, sinks, the kitchen or larder, a wash-house. Places which smell bad, prisons, places which bring unhappiness and lament, desolated places, places where scorpions or reptiles live. Wastebaskets, organic fertilizer stacks, garbage dumps, chemical laboratories, crematoriums, places where the deceased are bathed, and battlefields. According to al-Bīrūnī, it indicates vineyards and mulberry trees.[98]

Countries, Regions, and Cities: *Al-Qabīsī:* The Hijāz, the desert of the Arabs, districts in the direction of the Yemen, Tangier, Qumās, Rayy, and part of Sind. *Lilly:* Northern Bavaria, the woody part of Norway, Barbary, the kingdom of Fez, Catalonia, Valencia, Urbino, the Forum Julii in Italy, Vienna, Messina, Ghent, Frankfurt an der Oder. *H. S. Green:* Algeria, the Barbary Coast, Bavaria, Cappadocia, Catalonia, Judea, Jutland, Morocco, Norway, Queensland, Syria, Transvaal, Dover, East Grinstead, Glossop, Halifax, Hull, Liverpool, Newcastle, Stockport, Worthing, Baltimore, Cincinnati, Fez, Frankfurt an der Oder, Milwaukee, Messina, New Orleans, St. John's Newfoundland, Valencia, Washington. *Ivy M. Goldstein–Jacobson* adds: Baltimore, Canada, the Yukon.

SAGITTARIUS

Like the other fiery signs, Sagittarius represents hilly, sandy, and dry places which are not suitable for agriculture. According to Lilly, if Sagittarius is placed at the cusp of the 4th house in a horary chart for a question about buying land, the place is hilly, rocky and dry. Places represented by Sagittarius are of the nature of Jupiter and of the nature of the element of fire. Sagittarius, ruled by Jupiter, is also associated with places where foreigners live, religious places, and places related to international affairs.

Direction: East-southeast.

Places: A stable for great horses or horses for wars, or a house where usually great four-footed beasts are kept, fields, hills, and the highest places of lands or grounds that rise a little above the rest; in houses, upper rooms and near the fire.

---

[98] Al-Bīrūnī, §366.

Countries, Regions, and Cities: *Al-Qabīsī:* Baghdad, al-Jibāl, Isfahān, places of the Herpads[99] and fire worshippers, Ethiopia. *Lilly:* Spain, Hungary, Slavonia, Moravia, Dalmatia, Buda (in Hungary), Toledo, Narbonne, Cologne, Stargard (in Poland). *H. S. Green:* Arabia Felix,[100] Australia, Dalmatia, Western France from the Seine to Garonne Rivers over to Cape Finisterre (Spain), Hungary, Istria, Madagascar, Moravia, Provence, Slavonia, Spain, Tuscany, Bradford, West Bromwich, Nottingham, Sheffield, Sunderland, Avignon, Buda, Cologne, Narbonne, Rotenburg, Stuttgart, Taranto, Toledo. *Ivy M. Goldstein-Jacobson* adds: Yemen, Zanzibar.

CAPRICORN

The ancient astrologers associate Capricorn with agriculture and lands. According to Lilly, if Capricorn is placed at the cusp of the 4th house in a horary chart about land, then the place is plain, ideal for shepherds, or an ideal field for herding and cultivating. Places represented by Capricorn are of the nature of Saturn and the earthy element. As Saturn indicates dark colors and dark places, Capricorn also indicates desolate and dark places and the lower rooms of a house. Capricorn is related to building solid structures, and so Capricorn indicates castles, ports, warehouses, and dungeons. According to al-Bīrūnī, Capricorn is associated with places where slaves sleep, and the first part of the sign indicates stones and water wheels.[101]

Direction: South.

Places: An ox-house or cow-house or where calves are kept, or tools for husbandry, or where old wood is stored, or where sails for ships and such materials are stored; also sheep-pens and grounds

---

[99] **BD**: This is a class of Zoroastrian priests.
[100] **BD**: This is an old designation for parts of the Hijāz (western Saudi Arabia along the coast) and southern Arabia in and around Yemen.
[101] Al-Bīrūnī, §366.

where sheep feed, fallow grounds, barren fields which are bushy and thorny, dunghills in fields, or where soil is laid; in houses, low, dark places near the ground or threshold. Prisons, cells, dungeons, vaults, cellars, graves, deep hollows, caves, dark forests, frozen places, and goat pens are also related to Capricorn.

Countries, Regions, and Cities: *Al-Qabīsī:* Ethiopia, Mahrūbān, Sind, Oman as far as the sea, Hind. *Lilly:* Thrace, Macedonia, Albania, Bulgaria, southwest Saxony, the West Indies, Styria, the Orkney (Orcades) Islands, Hessia, Oxford, Mecklenburg, Cleves, Brandenburg. *H. S. Green:* Albania, Bosnia, Bulgaria, Macedonia, Illyria, Styria, Thrace, the Peloponnesian Peninsula, the "Circan,"[102] "Maracan," and Khurāsān regions of Iran, India, the Punjab, Afghanistan, Hesse, Mecklenburg, southwestern Saxony, Romandiola in Italy, Mexico, Orkney islands, Oxford, Salisbury, Keighley, Brandenburg, Brussels, Port Said, Prato in Tuscany, Constanz, Fayence in Provence, Tortona. *Ivy M. Goldstein–Jacobson* adds: Afghanistan, Alaska, Finland, Iceland, Mexico.

AQUARIUS

The ancient astrologers associate Aquarius with attics and roofs, as it is an airy sign, and also with rough places as it is ruled by Saturn. According to Lilly, if Aquarius is placed at the cusp of the 4th house in a horary chart for a question about buying land, the place is neither hilly nor flat, some of it is good and some not that good. As Aquarius means the "water-bearer," it is related to water, and as it is an air sign it is related to things that fly; consequently it indicates birds which live in waters and their shelters. As modern astrologers consider Uranus to be the lord of Aquarius, it is associated with technology and broadcasting stations. As uranium is named after Uranus, Aquarius is also associated with uranium.

---

[102] **BD**: Perhaps Jurjān.

Direction: West-northwest.

Places: Hilly and uneven places, places newly dug or where quarries of stone are, or any minerals which have been dug up; in houses the roof, eaves, or upper parts; vineyards, or near some little spring or conduit-head. It indicates running or still waters, heated bath water, taverns, brothels, channels and ditches, stockades, and shelters of birds that live in water.[103] Railroad crossings, stop signs, broadcasting stations (radio, TV), power lines, electric power units, uranium mines, garages, and conference rooms.

Countries, Regions, and Cities: *Al-Qabīsī:* The Sawād,[104] Kūfa and its district, the Hijāz, the land of the Copts in Egypt, western Sind. *Lilly:* Tartary, Croatia, Wallachia, Moscow, Westphalia, Piedmont (in Savoy), west and south Bavaria, Media, Arabia, Hamburg, Bremen, Montferrat and Pesaro (in Italy), Trent, Ingolstadt. *H. S. Green:* Abyssinia, Arabia Petraea,[105] the Causasus (Circassia), Lithuania, Piedmont, part of Poland, Prussia, Russia, Sweden, Tartary, Wallachia, Westphalia, Brighton, Salisbury, Bremen, Hamburg, Ingolstadt, Salzburg, Trent. *Ivy M. Goldstein–Jacobson* adds: Siberia.

PISCES

Being a watery sign, Pisces represents waters and places near water. According to Lilly, if Pisces is placed at the cusp of the 4th house in a horary chart for a question about buying land, the place is near water; there may be a river or lake near it. Jupiter, the traditional lord of this sign, represents abundant rains. Jupiter indicates divine matters and holy people, as they are also related to Pisces. Neptune, the modern lord of Pisces, is associated with waters and especially with seas. Oceans, fishing places, places

---

[103] Al-Bīrūnī, §366.
[104] **BD**: See the note for Taurus above.
[105] **BD**: This is an area around the southern Levant and the Sinai Peninsula.

underwater are also related to Pisces. Due to Neptune, Pisces is also related to oilfields and oil tanks. Being the twelfth sign, Pisces is associated with the 12th house and so indicates seclusion. Additionally, as Neptune is related to angelic and spiritual beings, Pisces is related to the domiciles of angels, miraculous people, and divine matters.

Direction: North-northwest.

Places : It represents places full of water, or where many springs and much fowl are, also fishponds or rivers full of fish, places where hermitages have been, moats about houses, watermills; in houses, near water (such as a well, pump, or where water stands). Fishing, places underwater, oceans, oilfields, spiritual places, necromancy sessions, and places where such sessions are held, ashrams. It also indicates the domiciles of angels, holy people, places of mourning, and seashores.[106]

Countries, Regions, and Cities: *Al-Qabīsī:* Tabaristān, the north of the land of Jurjān, part of the Byzantine Empire to Syria, al-Jazīrah, Egypt, Alexandria, the sea of Yemen.[107] *Lilly:* Calabria (in Sicily), Portugal, Normandy, northern Egypt, Alexandria, Rheims, Worms, Ratisbon, Compostela. *H. S. Green:* Calabria, Galicia in Spain, Normandy, Nubia, Portugal, Bournemouth, Christchurch, Cowes, Farnham, Grimsby, Lancaster, King's Lynn, Preston, Southport, Alexandria, Compostela, Ratisbon, Regensburg, Seville, Worms. *Ivy M. Goldstein–Jacobson* adds: Asia, Tiverton.

---

[106] Al-Bīrūnī, §366.
[107] **BD**: See footnote under Virgo.

5: CLASSIFICATION OF THE SIGNS

The signs are classified by certain characteristics which are then used in both natal and horary astrology. The following classification is based on Bonatti, who draws on al-Qabīsī.[108]

Rational (or human) signs: Gemini, Virgo, Libra, Aquarius, and the first half of Sagittarius. The symbols of these signs include human symbols. If the Moon or Ascendant is in the human signs, the native (or querent) is more rational, he also speaks more and better than others. Logic is important for people indicated by these signs; they think of the best way to reach their targets and act strategically. It is also said that these people have beautiful voices.

Winged signs: Gemini, Virgo, and Pisces.

Bestial or four-footed signs: Aries, Taurus, Leo, Capricorn, and the first half of Sagittarius. Aries, Taurus, and Capricorn are called "domestic" because they are represented by symbols of domestic animals. Bestial signs display a stronger sexual appetite than the other signs; they are motivated by their passions instead of logic, and act instinctively.

Fruitful or fertile signs: Cancer, Scorpio, and Pisces. Regarding questions on children, when the Ascendant, its lord, the lord of the 5th house, or the Moon is in fruitful signs, the native (or querent or quaesited) may have numerous children, if there is no affliction.

Unfruitful or less fruitful signs: Aries, Taurus, Libra, Sagittarius, Capricorn, and Aquarius. In questions about children, when the Ascendant, its lord, the lord of the 5th house, or the Moon is in these signs, the native may have fewer children.

---

[108] Bonatti, Tr. II.2, Ch. 20 (pp. 74-76); al-Qabīsī I.24.

Barren signs: Gemini, Leo, and Virgo. In questions about children, when the Ascendant, its lord, the lord of the 5th house, or the Moon is in barren signs, the native may be infertile.

Semi-voiced signs: Aries, Taurus, Leo, Capricorn (which are said to bleat, grunt, and roar), and the last half of Sagittarius. If the Ascendant, its lord, or the Moon is in one of these signs, the native (or perhaps, querent) talks very little and his speech is not fluent, unless these significators are influenced by positive factors.

Mute signs: Cancer, Scorpio, and Pisces. These signs are symbolized by mute animals. When the Ascendant, its lord, or the Moon is in one of these signs and not under any positive influence, the native may be silent or mute (or perhaps, very calm).

Signs of long and short (or straight and crooked) ascension: Signs of long ascension are from the beginning of Cancer to the end of Sagittarius, and take more than two hours to ascend on the horizon. Signs of short ascensions are from the beginning of Capricorn to the end of Gemini, and take less than two hours. (This is in the northern hemisphere: in the southern hemisphere, the categories are reversed.)

The above-mentioned classifications are widely used in horary astrology. If a person's significator is in one of the mute signs and a communication is needed to reach a solution in a certain matter, then we may expect that this person will keep silent at critical moments and will not express himself well enough. Or, in the same situation, if the querent's significator is one of the human signs, he would be a rational person who speaks much and better, and thinks of the best way to reach his goals and act strategically. If the querent's significator is in one of the fertile signs and the question is about pregnancy, then it is obvious that the answer will be positive. If the question is about financial issues, a significator in one of the fertile signs indicates prosperity. Fertility may also be considered to indicate mental productivity.

6: PRACTICAL ADVICE ON ANSWERING HORARY QUESTIONS

The masterpieces of ancient astrologers contain precious knowledge on how to answer horary questions. Rules of interpretation and the answers to example questions written in Arabic were compiled in their Latin translation by Guido Bonatti in his famous work *Liber Astronomiae* (*The Book of Astronomy*).[109] These kinds of compilations were helpfully classified by house topic, so astrologers could consult the relevant house for their question and find the standard rules. William Lilly, who lived a few centuries after Bonatti, likewise compiled the rules of his predecessors in this way in *Christian Astrology* Volume II, with numerous chart examples. Below I will do something of the same, classifying questions based on houses and offering useful hints for answering them.

QUESTIONS ON 1ST HOUSE MATTERS

Here I will address some hints for answering questions about health issues, the benefit of any matter, and finding a lost person.

Health issues

When a querent asks about health or survival, we should examine the Ascendant, the lord of the Ascendant or the Moon, and see if it is afflicted or not. This affliction includes: being burned or combust, being in conjunction, square, or opposition with a malefic planet, or a conjunction with the South Node.

When the lord of the Ascendant or the Moon is burned or under the rays, this indicates there is a problem with the health. The possibility is higher if those significators apply to the Sun or if the Sun

---

[109] Bonatti, Tr. VI.

is applying to the lord of the Ascendant (which is in turn slower in motion than the Sun). This means the illness will get worse and the querent will have a health problem.

Aspects of the lord of the Ascendant and the Moon with the house lords are also important. If the lord of the Ascendant or the Moon is in square, opposition, or conjunction with the lord of the 8th, 12th, 6th, or 4th house, we may conclude that there is a health problem. In particular, the lord of the 6th or 8th in detriment indicates that the querent will have some health problems, and if there are other negative indicators he will be open to risks and even vital dangers.

The lord of the Ascendant or the Moon in good houses like the 1st, 11th, and 10th, is a positive indicator of health.

The lord of the Ascendant in direct motion, in its essential dignity, quick in motion, or in one of the angular houses, is a positive indicator about the querent's health. The lord of the Ascendant or the Moon in conjunction, sextile, or trine with Venus or Jupiter is also a positive indicator.

To identify when the health problems will emerge, or when risky and dangerous situations will come to the surface, we should consider when the lord of the Ascendant or the Moon will reach the point of burning or a harmful aspect. Using the symbolic timing methods we saw in Chapter 2, if for instance any of these significators makes an exact conjunction or aspect within 5°, the expected development takes place after a period of 5 time units, depending on the types of signs and what seems reasonable for the querent's situation. However, other factors should also be considered: significators in angular houses speed up the developments. The degree of a cusp which the significator is about to reach may be considered: if a malefic is 5° behind the cusp of the 6th house, this distance may be considered for predicting the timing.

The lord of the Ascendant or the Moon in the 6th house is one of the indicators for illness. If the lord of the 6th is in the 8th, the illness may turn out to be risky. If the lord of the Ascendant is weaker than the lord of the 6th house, illness prevails. If the lord of the Ascendant is in the 6th, 8th, or 12th, the health of the querent is under threat. If the lord of the 6th or 8th is in the 1st, the querent is exposed to diseases and risks related to his health.

General rule: Where the damage comes from may be understood by considering the houses ruled by the planets which make negative aspects with the Ascendant, the lord of the Ascendant, or the Moon.

If the Ascendant, its lord, or the Moon is in contact with one of the malefic fixed stars, the querent experiences health problems; or, if the querent is worried about the acceleration of those problems, this may be true.

If the significator makes a conjunction, sextile, or trine with a benefic before reaching an exact negative aspect, the querent will have the chance to recover before health problems increase. William Lilly states about such aspects: "Medicine or strength of Nature will contradict that malignant influence."[110]

Geographical directions

Each quadrant of a horary chart indicates a certain direction. The 1st house represents the beginning of the east. When we move in a clockwise direction, between the 1st and 10th corresponds to east. South begins with the 10th, and between the 10th and the 7th house is the south. West starts with the 7th, and between the 7th and the 4th house is the west. The 4th house represents the beginning of the north, and between the 4th and 1st house is the north.

The quadrant where Jupiter, Venus, and the Lot of Fortune are placed is considered to be the field of life where the querent will attain luck and profit. However, if Jupiter or Venus is the lord of the 6th, 8th, or 10th, this may lead to misfortune. Then the querent

---

[110] Lilly, p. 132.

is advised he should avoid being in the regions represented by the houses where those significators are placed. In the regions represented by the houses where Saturn and Mars are placed, the querent may experience some difficulties and problems. So, those places are not favored. The quadrant where the lord of the Ascendant and the Moon are placed is also a significator for determining the region that the querent may live in or travel to.

Past and future events

The most recent and the next aspects of the lord of the Ascendant and the Moon are important in a horary chart. Past aspects indicate events which took place before the question, and the next aspect indicates what will take place after it. The aspects of the lord of the Ascendant and the Moon, the characteristics of the planets they aspect, and the houses they rule, should also be evaluated.

"Is it beneficial?"

When some news or an offer is received, we may erect a chart to see if it is beneficial or not, based on the moment it is heard. Then the aspects of the lord of the Ascendant and the Moon are considered. If one of them is applying by sextile or trine with the Sun, Jupiter, or Venus, the news or offer is beneficial. On the other hand if one of them is applying to a conjunction, square, or opposition with Mars or Saturn, the news or offer is not beneficial. The lord of the Ascendant or the Moon applying to a conjunction with the North Node indicates it is beneficial, whereas the South Node is not beneficial. If one of those significators is entering into burning or is burned it is not beneficial; if applying to the Lot of Fortune, it is beneficial and fortunate. Application to the square or opposition of Mercury may indicate misinformation.

If the lord of the Ascendant or the Moon is afflicted, the source of the damage comes from the house the planet is in, or the house it rules. For instance, if the lord of the Ascendant or the Moon is afflicted by a malefic who is in the 11th or is the lord of the 11th, the friends will cause some restrictions or difficulties. When other planets (besides Mars, Saturn, and the South Node) have hard aspects to the Moon or the lord of the Ascendant, it will not be as difficult as the malefics but there still will be some conflicts and disagreements if there is no reception between that planet and the Moon or the lord of the Ascendant. But if the Moon or the lord of the Ascendant is in a good aspect with a planet which is in the 11th or rules it, or if they are in hard aspects with the benefics but with reception, then friends will help to bring the matter to perfection, and they will work for a common good. The accomplishment of what is desired will be easy, and there will be success without much effort.

Finding a Lost Person

When such a question is asked, first of all we should understand the relationship between the querent and the lost person (the quaesited). If there is no relationship between the querent and the quaesited, then the Ascendant, the planets in the 1st, the lord of the Ascendant, and the Moon represent the quaesited or missing person. If the querent has a relationship with the quaesited, then we should first determine this relationship and derive houses relative to the Ascendant. For instance, if the querent asks about his own missing sibling, then the 3rd house, the planets in it, the lord of the 3rd, and the Moon, represent the quaesited. If the missing person is the child of the querent, then the lord of the 5th house is the significator of the quaesited. If this lord is in the 6th, 8th, or 12th of the horary chart, or if it is in conjunction, square, or opposition with the malefics (Mars and Saturn), or in a conjunction with the South Node, the quaesited may have some health problems or be dead. The same opinion may be rendered if those significators are in the 6th, 8th, or 12th house relative to the house which the quaesited is assigned to. But if the significator is in one of the strong houses, then the quaesited is healthy and well.

If the significator is in the 9th, the quaesited is far away; if in the 3rd or 1st, the quaesited is nearby. If the significator of the quaesited is retrograde, it indicates that the quaesited may return.

If the querent is worried about the life or death of a missing person and there is no relationship between the querent and quaesited, then the 8th house, planets in it, and the lord of that house are considered. The lord of the Ascendant or the Moon is evaluated based on their relationship with those planets. If the querent has a relationship with the quaesited, such as if the missing person is the querent's sibling, then the 8th and 10th (and planets in them, and their lords) should be considered together: the 8th because it is the natural house of death, and the 10th because it is the 8th house from the 3rd (i.e., the sibling's death). If the lord of the Ascendant or the lord of the derived Ascendant (such as the lord of the 3rd) makes an inharmonious aspect with the lord of the 8th or the derived 8th (in this case, the lord of the 10th), or if it is afflicted by the malefics or entering into burning, the missing person may be dead.

QUESTIONS ON 2ND HOUSE MATTERS

Here I will give practical advice on monetary issues generally, and lending and borrowing.

Monetary issues in general

As with all questions, the significators of the querent are the Ascendant, the lord of the Ascendant, and the Moon. Since the question is related to monetary issues, we should evaluate the sign at the cusp of the 2nd, planets in the 2nd, the lord of the 2nd, and the condition of the Moon, to determine the quaesited. The house and sign of the Lot of Fortune and its lord should also be evaluated.

The first thing to do is see if the lord of the Ascendant or the Moon makes any aspect with the lord of the 2nd, and if so, what aspect it is. If there is no aspect between them, we should look for reception; if there is no reception, we should look for an antiscial and contra-antiscial relation.

The significators of money (the lord of the 2nd, the Lot of Fortune and its lord) in angular houses, in their essential dignities, in direct and quick movement, indicate a positive financial situation. If the lord of the 2nd or the lord of the Lot is in the 1st house, the querent may attain the financial power or money he desires. The conjunction, sextile, and trine of the lord of the Ascendant with the lord of the 2nd, the Lot and/or its lord, or Jupiter or Venus, also points out positive developments in financial issues. The lord of the 2nd house in conjunction with benefic fixed stars like Regulus, Spica, and Betelgeuse brings the same influence. The North Node in the 2nd house or the lord of the 2nd house in conjunction with the North Node, also indicates positive developments in financial issues and monetary power.

The house where the lord of the 2nd is placed is important: it shows the area where the querent will earn money.

If the lord of the 2nd is in the 1st, the querent earns money through his own efforts and talents, and more easily than he expects.

If the lord of the 2nd house is in the 9th, the querent earns money from international affairs, business with foreigners, and through education and travel. We may do the same with the other houses and determine the source of income. The sign and house where the Lot of Fortune is, and the sign and the house where its lord is placed, also give us information about this issue.

If the Lot of Fortune is in the 5th, the income is created through activities related to children and creative activities; in the 7th, through the spouse or partners; in the 11th, through friends and social organizations; in the 3rd, through siblings, close relatives or neighbors, communication skills and travels; in the 2nd, through the querent's success in managing his own wealth, or his business ventures; in the 5th, through gambling, sports, artistic abilities and performing arts, children, brokerage, hobbies, and through wealth inherited from the querent's father.

The conjunction, trine, and sextile of the lord of the 2nd house with the benefics or the Lot of Fortune brings positive results in terms of earnings. The aspects of the lord of the 2nd are also important. If the lord of the 2nd is in a harmonious aspect with the lord of the 10th, the querent earns money through people in authority, nobles, bosses and managers, or through business affairs or in the public arena.

Inharmonious aspects between the lord of the 2nd and other planets should also be considered. If that planet is the lord of the 3rd, the querent's siblings or close relatives may create difficulties or obstacles for the querent's earnings. If the lord of the 2nd is in a hard aspect with the lord of the 7th, the querent's spouse or partner brings problems. If the lord of the 2nd is in hard aspect with the lord of the 1st, the querent himself is the obstacle.

The house where the South Node is placed should also be considered, since the South Node restricts or damages the potentials of the house it is in. If it is in the 8th, the querent may have losses due to joint ventures; if in the 10th, the querent may have losses due to the illegal practices of the bosses or the querent himself.

Lending and Borrowing

The lord of the Ascendant and the Moon represent the querent, the lord of the 2nd represents the querent's budget. The 7th and its lord represent the person from whom the querent wants to borrow money (the quaesited), while the 8th and its lord represent the money of the quaesited. If the lord of the Ascendant or the lord of the 2nd is in conjunction, sextile, or trine with the lord of the 8th or a planet in it, the querent gets or borrows the money he wants. On the other hand, if there are inharmonious aspects between the significators (if the lord of the Ascendant or 2nd is in conjunction, square, or opposition with the malefics, or applies to conjunction with the South Node), the querent cannot get or borrow the money he wants.

If the lord of the 8th is in the 1st or 2nd houses, or if there is a harmonious aspect between the lord of the 2nd and the lord of the 8th (or if they are in conjunction), the querent gets what he wants. The Lot of Fortune or its lord in the 1st also indicates the same thing.

If the querent's wish is related to an authority figure, boss, or the government, the 10th and its lord represent the quaesited. The 11th house, which is the 2nd from the 10th, represents the money or financial situation of the quaesited. If the lord of the Ascendant or the Moon is in a harmonious aspect or conjunction with the lord of the 10th or 11th, the querent gets the financial support from the quaesited (who is a person in authority). On the other hand, if the lord of the Ascendant or the Moon is in an inharmonious aspect with the lord of the 10th or 11th, or unaspected, the querent cannot get the financial support from the quaesited. The lord of the 11th being placed in the 1st is a positive indicator, showing that the desired outcome is likely.

By determining the planet which blocks the desired outcome (the planet which is in an inharmonious aspect with the significator of the querent or the quaesited), the house which this planet is in and the house(s) it rules, indicate who or what causes the obstacles and in which field of life they will be experienced.

QUESTIONS ON 3ʳᴰ HOUSE MATTERS

Under this heading I deal with siblings and close relatives, rumors and news, and journeys.

Siblings and close relatives

If the question is about siblings, the lord of the Ascendant and the Moon represent the querent, the 3ʳᵈ house and its lord the quaesited (the sibling, close relative, or neighbor). If the question pertains to relatives, harmonious aspects between the lord of the Ascendant and the lord of the 3ʳᵈ bring positive relations with the quaesited. The same influence is valid for harmonious aspects between the lord of the 3ʳᵈ house and the Moon or the rising degree. If the lord of the Ascendant is in the 3ʳᵈ house, the querent strives to find concord with his siblings or relatives; likewise when the lord of the 3ʳᵈ is in the 1ˢᵗ, the siblings or relatives try to find concord with the querent.

If the malefics (Mars, Saturn, South Node) are in the 3ʳᵈ house at the time of the question, the querent is not supported by his siblings or his inner circle, especially if Mars and Saturn are not in their own dignities. If Venus, Jupiter, or the North Node is in the 3ʳᵈ, the querent is supported by his siblings and inner circle.

If the lord of the Ascendant or the Moon is applying to a conjunction, square, or opposition of malefics, the querent is harmed due to his siblings and inner circle; if one of those significators are applying to a sextile or trine with benefics, the querent is supported by them.

"Is the rumor true?"

The 3ʳᵈ house, the Moon, and Mercury are considered for such questions. If the benefics are in the 3ʳᵈ, or if the lord of the 3ʳᵈ or the Moon is applying to a conjunction, sextile, or trine of the benefics, the rumor is true. The Moon being void in course indicates that the rumor is false. The rumor is false when the Moon and Mercury are in inharmonious aspects.

The benefics in the 1st indicate that the rumor is true or the offer is a beneficial one. On the other hand, if Mars or Saturn is in the 1st, the rumor is false and the offer is a bad one. The applying harmonious aspect of the lord of the Ascendant with Jupiter, Venus, or the Sun, indicates that the rumor is true. Its conjunction, square, or opposition with Saturn or Mars, as well as a conjunction with the South Node, indicates that the rumor is false.

If the axes of the chart are on fixed signs, if the Moon and Mercury are also in fixed signs, and if they are not affected by the above negative conditions, the rumor is true.

If Jupiter, Venus, the Sun, or the North Node is in the 10th, the news or the offer is beneficial for the future of the querent. On the other hand, Saturn, Mars, or the South Node in the 10th indicates that it is not beneficial.

Lee Lehman listed the possible arguments for the question "Is the rumor true?" which she compiled from the works of William Lilly and from Gadbury, in her *The Martial Art of Horary*.[111]

Indications of a true rumor:
- The lord of the Ascendant, the Moon, or the Moon's lord (or the majority of them) in fixed signs, not cadent, and in good aspect to the benefics or the Sun.
- All four angles in fixed signs, likewise the Moon and Mercury, and they in turn are separating from malefics and applying to an angular benefic.
- The MC/IC axis in fixed signs, and the Moon ruling either angle.

---

[111] Lehman, pp. 87-88.

- The Moon in the 1st, 3rd, 10th, or 11th, separating from a good aspect to any planet and applying by a good aspect to the lord of the Ascendant.

Indications of a false or misleading rumor:
- The lord of the Ascendant, the Moon, or the lord of the Moon cadent and afflicted by malefics (whether or not they are in good zodiacal condition).
- Benefics in the 1st, but the Moon unfortunate.
- Mercury retrograde or debilitated.
- The planet to whom the Moon or Mercury next applies, being afflicted.
- The Moon either void in course or in a bad aspect to Mercury.
- The Moon square or opposite Mercury, neither one being in a good aspect to the Ascendant.

Other indications:
- The lord of the Ascendant or the Moon under the rays indicates secrecy in the matter.
- If the lord of the 6th, 8th, or 12th is in the 1st, or afflicting the lord of the Ascendant, or Mars or Saturn is retrograde and in the 1st, or in a bad aspect to either the ascending degree or the lord of the Ascendant, the querent will receive damage or prejudice from the news.

Questions about journeys

For short distance journeys, the 3rd house should be considered, whereas the 9th house should be reserved for long distance journeys. For questions about short journeys, if Saturn, Mars, or the South Node is in the 3rd, if the lord of the 3rd or the Moon is applying to the conjunction, square, or opposition of Saturn, Mars, or the South Node, the querent's journey will not be good, he will not benefit from this journey, or he will face some risks during it. For long journeys, if Saturn, Mars, or the South Node is in the 9th, if the lord of the 9th or the Moon is applying to the conjunction, square, or opposition of Saturn, Mars, or the South Node, the querent's journey will not be good, he will not benefit from this journey, or he will face some risks during it. The lord of the Ascendant being slow in motion indicates that the journey will begin within a short time or it will progress quickly.

QUESTIONS ON 4TH HOUSE MATTERS

This advice concerns questions about hidden or mislaid items, buying and selling houses and lands, and moving to another place.

Hidden or mislaid items

First we should determine to whom the mislaid or hidden item belongs. For instance, if the mislaid item belongs to the querent, querent is the 1st and the item the 2nd; but if it belongs to the querent's sibling, the sibling is the 3rd and the item the 4th (the 2nd from the 3rd); if to the querent's child, the child is the 5th and the item the 6th (the 2nd from it); if to the spouse, the spouse is the 7th and the item the 8th (the 2nd from it).

Using the querent himself as the model, if the lord of the 2nd is in one of the angular houses, then the missing item may be somewhere near the querent, probably where the querent is, or among the things that the querent frequently uses. This is more significant when the lord of the 2nd house is actually in the 1st house. If the lord of the 2nd is in the 10th, the missing item is somewhere in the querent's office; if it is in the 7th the item is in a place belonging to the querent's spouse; if it is in the 4th the item is in the querent's house, somewhere that the querent often uses.

If the mislaid item is a precious one, we should also look to the house and the sign where the Lot of Fortune is.

We should also consider the element of the sign on the 2nd house, the sign in which the lord of the 2nd house is, and the sign of the Lot and its lord. If most of these significators are in watery signs, the lost item is in a place which is wet, damp, or near water. In a house this may be the kitchen or bathroom. If the majority of the significators are in fiery signs, the lost item is near heat such as the oven, fireplace, or any kind of heater. If most of the significators are in earthy signs, the lost item is near the ground or the earth, or in or under a flowerpot. If most of the significators are in airy signs, the lost item is in an airy place, like somewhere near the air conditioner.

William Lilly uses a slightly different approach. First he considers the ascending sign, its nature, and the quarter of heaven it signifies (such as a fiery sign indicating the east). Secondly, he considers what sign the lord of the Ascendant is in, the sign of the 4th, and the sign the lord of the 4th house is in, what sign the Moon is in, the sign in the 2nd house and the sign the lord of the 2nd house is in, the sign which the Lot of Fortune is in and what quarter of the heaven this sign signifies. Then, based on the greatest number of testimonies, he predicts the place of the missing or lost item.[112] Following is his list of the cardinal directions for each sign, organized by triplicity:

♈: East; ♌: East-northeast; ♐: East-southeast.
♎: West; ♊: West-southwest; ♒: West-northwest.
♋: North; ♏: North-northeast; ♓: North-northwest.
♑: South; ♉: South-southeast; ♍: South-southwest.

If the significator of the lost item (the lord of the 2nd house or the lord of the Lot of Fortune) is approaching a conjunction or harmonious aspect with the lord of the Ascendant, or if the Moon

---

[112] Lilly, p. 204.

is transferring the light to a conjunction or harmonious aspect between those two, the querent finds what he has lost. If there is a square or opposition, or a reception between these two significators, the querent finds what he has lost after some difficulties and effort.

Buying and selling lands or houses

The Ascendant and its lord represent the querent (whether buyer or seller), the 7th and its lord represent the other party. The Moon and the 4th house and its lord represent the house or the land that will be bought or sold. The 10th and its lord represent the price of the house or land.

If there is an approaching harmonious aspect or conjunction between the lord of the Ascendant and the lord of the 7th, the buyer and seller will reach an agreement. If there is no approaching aspect between these two, but the Moon is transferring the light between them by a conjunction or harmonious aspect, the same thing is valid. If the approaching aspect between the lord of the Ascendant and the lord of the 7th is an inharmonious one, the buyer and the seller cannot reach an agreement. If there is no approaching aspect between the lord of the Ascendant and the lord of the 7th, but the Moon is transferring the light between them by a conjunction or inharmonious aspect, the buyer and the seller cannot reach an agreement.

The lord of the Ascendant in the 7th house represents that the querent is bargaining or he is bound to the conditions of the other party. That means the other party has advantage. The lord of the 7th in the 1st means that the conditions of the other party are bound to the querent: so the querent, represented by the 1st house, has the advantage.

If there is a conjunction or harmonious aspect between the lord of the Ascendant and the lord of the 4th, or a harmonious aspect between the Moon and the lord of the 4th, the querent buys or sells the house that he asks the question about.

If Saturn, Mars, or the South Node is placed in the 4th house, the house or land that will be bought or sold is in a bad condition. If Jupiter, Venus, or the North Node is placed in the 4th, the house or land is in a good condition. If the lord of the 4th or the Moon is applying to the conjunction, square, or opposition of Saturn or Mars or to conjunction with the South Node, problems related to that house or land may come to the surface. Buying the house might not be a good decision.

For a question related to the price of the house or land, the 10th house and its lord should be considered. If the lord of the 10th is in one of the angular houses, if it is in its dignity, not retrograde, the price of the house or land is expensive. If the lord of the 10th is in one of the cadent houses, not in its dignity, or is retrograde or afflicted by the malefics, the price is cheap.

The same rules apply to rental situations.

"Is it good to move to another house, or stay in place?"

The house that the querent currently lives in, is represented by the 4th house and its lord. The house that he will move to is represented by the 7th house and its lord. Whether the benefics or malefics are placed in these houses, or whether their lords apply to an aspect with the malefics and the benefics, should be considered. For instance, if Saturn or the South Node is placed in the 4th, the querent does not feel comfortable in the house he is living in.

The same influence is valid when the lord of the 4th house is applying to the conjunction, square, or opposition with Mars or Saturn, or applying to a conjunction with the South Node, or entering into burning. If Jupiter, Venus, or the South Node is in the 7th, then moving to another place would be better. The same influence is valid when the lord of the 7th is applying to a conjunction or harmonious aspect with Venus, Jupiter, or the North Node. The lord of the 1st or the 4th placed in the 7th may indicate the querent will move to another place.

If fixed signs are on the axes of the chart and the Moon is also in a fixed sign, the querent does not move. If cardinal or mutable signs are on the axes and the Moon is in a cardinal or mutable sign, the querent moves.

On this issue, William Lilly states: "If the Moon separate at [the] time of the Question from Jupiter or Venus, then stay; if she separate from an *Infortune*, remove; or a *Fortune* in the ascendant bids you stay; an *Infortune* remove."[113]

QUESTIONS ON 5TH HOUSE MATTERS

Here I address questions related to pregnancy, children, mediators and brokers, and the paternal inheritance.

Whether the querent will have children

For answering such questions, the sign on the 5th house, the lord of the 5th, or the aspect between the Moon and the lord of the 5th should be considered. Harmonious applying aspects between these significators show that the querent will have a child. If the aspects between the significators are inharmonious but they are in mutual reception, the querent will have a baby after dealing with some obstacles and delays.

According to William Lilly the lord of the Ascendant or the Moon in the 5th house is a positive indicator of having a child. Even if there is no major aspect between the lord of the Ascendant and the lord of the 5th, if the Moon links those two through an applying aspect, the querent will have a child. Similarly, if a slower

---

[113] Lilly, pp. 213-214.

planet is collecting the light of the lord of the Ascendant and the lord of the 5th house, the querent will get pregnant.[114]

Benefics in the 5th house (Jupiter, Venus, and the North Node) are positive indicators that the querent will have a child, whereas malefics (Saturn, Mars, South Node) in that house are negative indicators.

The lord of the 5th in the 1st shows that the querent will have a child. On the other hand, the lord of the 5th applying to a conjunction, square, or opposition of a malefic (Mars or Saturn), or a conjunction with the South Node, indicates the opposite.

Benefics on the Ascendant, or with the lord of the 5th house or the lord of the Ascendant, or the lord of the 5th house in the 7th house, indicate that conception will occur or there is already a pregnancy. If all of those combinations include malefic planets with malefic aspects or the conjunction, the opposite is true. However, if the question is not whether the querent will get pregnant now or at a specific time, but if she will *ever* get pregnant, the querent's natal chart should be considered.

The lord of the 5th house placed in the 6th, 8th, or 12th houses, or in a negative aspect with the planets that rule these houses (or with malefics) means that the pregnancy may be a difficult one or there may be a risk or abortion.

The timing of the pregnancy

If the querent wants to know when she will get pregnant, the general condition of the lord of the 5th house is considered. In a chart that promises pregnancy, if the lord of the 5th house is quick in motion then the pregnancy will occur quickly. A retrograde or slow-moving 5th house lord indicates a delay in pregnancy. If the lord of the 5th is in one of the angular houses, pregnancy will occur quickly; if is in one of the succedents, pregnancy will occur in the

---

[114] Lilly, pp. 225-226.

medium term; if in one of the cadents, pregnancy will occur with a delay. The lord of the 5th in one of the cardinal signs speeds up pregnancy. If the lord of the 5th is in one of the mutable signs, pregnancy occurs in the medium term; if in one of the fixed signs, in the long term. If the lord of the 5th is in one of the mutable signs but is quick and in direct motion, and safe from restricting aspects, then pregnancy occurs quickly.

The lord of the 5th, the Moon, or the lord of the Ascendant in conjunction, square, or opposition with Saturn indicates obstacles or delay in pregnancy. When this aspect becomes exact (by converting the degrees into days, months, or years), the querent or the quaesited experiences some obstacles related to pregnancy.

Any benefics (Jupiter, Venus, the Lot of Fortune, or the North Node) in the 5th house and their positive aspects may speed up the timing of the pregnancy. The querent may get pregnant sooner than she expects. On the other hand, any malefics (Saturn, Mars, or the South Node) in the 5th house and their negative aspect may delay the pregnancy.

The lord of the 5th or a planet in it being retrograde, may indicate pregnancy will occur with a delay.

Positive significators for pregnancy

The lord of the Ascendant in a strong position, especially in one of the angular houses, and the Moon in one of the angular houses, are positive indicators about pregnancy.

The harmonious aspect of the Moon or one of the benefics with a planet placed in the 5th indicates the querent will have a baby.

If the lord of the Ascendant makes a conjunction with the lord of the 5th in one of the angular houses, and they are not afflicted by the benefics nor burned, those indicators show that the querent will have a baby.

The Moon or the lord of the 5th approaching an aspect with Jupiter or Venus, or being with the North Node, or approaching a conjunction with the Lot of Fortune, increases the possibility of having a baby. On the other hand the Moon or the lord of the 5th approaching a conjunction, square, or opposition with Mars or Saturn, or a conjunction with the South Node, may prevent pregnancy or increase the risk of miscarriage. Other negative significators increase this possibility.

The sex of the children

To answer the question asked by a pregnant woman "is my baby a girl or a boy?" we should consider the genders of the signs in which the significators are placed. Masculine signs represent the possibility of a boy, while feminine signs represent a girl. The significators include: the sign on the Ascendant, the sign in which the lord of the Ascendant is placed, the sign in which the lord of the 5th is placed, the sign where the Moon is, the sign in which the lord of the Moon is placed, and the sign in which the lord of the hour is placed. If most of those significators are in masculine signs, it is predicted that the baby is a boy. If the most of the significators are in feminine signs then it is predicted the baby is a girl. (Masculine signs are Aries, Gemini, Leo, Libra, Sagittarius and Aquarius. Feminine signs are Taurus, Cancer, Virgo, Scorpio, Capricorn and Pisces.)

When such a question is asked, we should consider whether the planet which the Moon next aspects, is in a masculine or feminine sign. If the other significators are scattered in masculine and feminine signs and the astrologer is indecisive in answering the question, the gender of the planet the Moon next aspects should be considered. If the Moon is approaching a planet which is in a masculine sign, the baby is a boy; if it is approaching a planet which is in a feminine sign, then it is a girl.

The gender of the planet in the 5th house and/or the next aspects of the Moon should also be considered. Saturn, Jupiter, Mars, and the Sun are masculine; Venus and Moon are feminine.

Mercury is considered masculine when he is in contact with a masculine planet and feminine when in contact with a feminine one. Mercury is also considered masculine if he is eastern, but feminine if western.

The health of the mother and child

If the querent is asking about the baby's health during or after the pregnancy, the 5th house, the lord of the 5th, and the Moon are considered. Additionally, the 6th and 8th houses of the horary chart, the 6th house from the 5th by derived houses (which means the 10th), and the 8th house from the 5th (which is the 12th) should also be considered.

If the Moon or the lord of the 5th makes a conjunction, square, or opposition with the benefics, or if any of them is approaching a conjunction with the South Node, or is retrograde, burned, or in one of the cadent houses, the baby's health is not in a good condition. Malefic significators (Saturn, Mars, and the South Node) in the 1st house do not bode well. Likewise, negative aspects between the lord of the 5th house and the lord of the 6th or 8th of the horary chart, or with the lord of the 6th house from the 5th (that is, the 10th) or the lord of the 8th house, do not bode well either. If the lord of the 5th is in the 6th and afflicted, the child may have some health problems; if the lord of the 5th is in the 8th and afflicted, the child's life may be under threat.

If the question is about the mother's health after birth, the planets that the Moon will first make an aspect with, and the type of aspect, should be considered. If the Moon is applying to a conjunction, sextile, or trine with a planet, the mother's health will be fine. An approaching aspect with a planet in its own dignity, in a strong position and in one of the angular houses, also brings a positive prediction. If the Moon makes a square or opposition to Jupiter or Venus, this position does not represent a health problem unless one of them is the lord of the 6th or the 8th. If the Moon is approaching a conjunction, square, or opposition with Mars or Saturn, or a conjunction with the South Node, or a negative aspect with the lord of the 6th or 8th, it represents negative conditions related to the mother's health.

"Will she have twins?"

For questions regarding twins, the significators in the double-bodied signs (Gemini, Virgo, Sagittarius, and Pisces) are considered. Any double-bodied sign on the Ascendant and/or in the 5th house, the Moon in any double-bodied sign, the lord of the Moon in any double-bodied sign, the lord of the 5th house in any double-bodied sign, and the lord of the hour in any double-bodied sign, indicates the querent will have twins.

"When will a pregnancy occur?"

For this question, the approaching aspects of the main significator should be considered. The main criterion is the number of degrees for the Moon or the lord of the 5th to make an exact aspect with the planet in front of it. If this aspect is in one of the cardinal signs the pregnancy occurs quickly; if in one of the mutable signs it occurs in the medium term; if in one of the fixed signs it occurs over the long term. If the significators make such an aspect in one of the angular houses the pregnancy occurs quickly; in the succedent houses, in the medium term; in the cadent houses, over the long term.

If there is not an approaching aspect between these significators, then consider when the lord of the 5th or the Moon makes an exact aspect with the lord of the hour. By calculating the future date when this transiting aspect will become exact, the time of conception may be predicted.

In the horary chart the degree of the Lot of children should also be calculated. If one of the benefics, the lord of the Ascendant, the lord of the 5th, or the Moon is approaching an aspect or conjunction with this point, the future time when this aspect will reach exactness in real time is calculated and the prediction is made accordingly. The formula for Lot of children is:

<u>Diurnal</u>: Ascendant + Saturn - Jupiter (from Jupiter to Saturn, projected from Ascendant)
<u>Nocturnal</u>: Ascendant + Jupiter – Saturn (from Saturn to Jupiter, projected from Ascendant)

There are also two different formulas or Lots for the sex of the children: the Lot of daughters and Lot of sons. Both of these points should be calculated in the horary chart and their lords should be taken into consideration. By determining the strongest of these lords and their positions, prediction on the sex of the child is made:

<u>Lot of daughters</u>: Ascendant + Venus - Moon (from Moon to Venus, projected from Ascendant)

<u>Lot of sons</u>: Ascendant + Jupiter – Moon (from Moon to Jupiter, projected from Ascendant)

In addition to calculating when the applying aspect will reach exact point, an ephemeris may also be used. For instance, let's assume Gemini is rising and Libra is on the cusp of the 5th house; moreover, Mercury (the lord of the Ascendant), is applying to conjunction with Venus (the lord of the 5th). The prediction may be made by calculating the degrees needed for an exact conjunction, or through looking at ephemeris or astrology software for the exact time of this conjunction in real time (which is a secondary method). For such a question, if the lord of the Ascendant or the Moon is close to the cusp of the 5th house, one may make a prediction by counting the degrees. Similarly, if the lord of the

Ascendant, the Moon, or the lord of the 5th is at the end of its sign and about to enter the next one, the prediction may be made based on the time of changing signs.

"Will my relationship with my son or daughter improve?"

The main significators that will help us answer this question are the lord of the Ascendant, the lord of the 5th, and the Moon. A conjunction, sextile, or trine between the lord of the Ascendant and the lord of the 5th or the Moon, or transferring the light of those two through a positive aspect or conjunction, indicates that the querent's relationship with his children will improve. The same is valid when a planet which is slower than the lord of the Ascendant and the lord of the 5th is collecting the light of these two significators.

The lord of the Ascendant, the lord of the 5th, and the Moon applying to an aspect with a benefic or any benefics in the 1st or 5th houses, also shows that the querent's relationship with his children will improve. On the other hand, the lord of the Ascendant, the lord of the 5th, or the Moon applying to a conjunction or negative aspect with a malefic in the 1st or 5th houses shows that the relationship between the querent and his children will get worse.

In addition to the benefics (Jupiter, Venus, North Node), the above-mentioned main significators applying to an aspect with a dignified planet may also be considered a positive indicator. For instance, benefics applying to an aspect with a dignified Mercury shows that the querent's dialogue with his child will improve.

Benefics in the 1st house of the horary chart indicate that the querent is right-minded and trying to improve the situation. When malefics are in the 1st, the querent may behave in a repressive (Saturn) or harsh (Mars) manner towards his child. When malefics or benefics are placed in the 5th, they may relate to the attitude of the querent's child. Malefics in the 5th suggest that the child is ill-minded or problematic; he may be rebellious and combative (Mars) or cold and distant (Saturn).

Mediators and brokers

As the 5th house also relates to mediators and middle-men, it should be considered for questions relating to mediators and brokers.[115] The buyer and seller in transactions or in business deals are represented by the 1st and 7th houses. The person who mediates between the two parties is represented by the lord of the 5th, planets in the 5th, and the Moon.

The lord of the 5th being in positive aspect with the lord of the Ascendant and the lord of the 7th show that the mediator will do his duty for the parties and help the deal. On the other hand, the lord of the 5th house applying to an inharmonious aspect with the lord of the Ascendant and the lord of the 7th shows the mediator will not be successful or will make trouble. Similarly, if the Moon transfers the light of the lord of the Ascendant and the lord of the 7th through a negative aspect, or if a slower third planet is in negative aspects with the lord of the Ascendant and the lord of the 7th, the mediator will not be successful.

If the lord of the 5th house (representing the mediator) is applying to a negative aspect with the lord of the 2nd (the finances of the querent), the mediator may create financial problems for the querent: the querent may pay more for the thing he bought, or he may pay more in commissions than he should. However, if the lord of the 5th is applying by a positive aspect to the lord of the 2nd (or the lord of the 2nd applies by a positive aspect to the lord of the 5th), the mediator or the broker will have a positive influence on the querent's budget. For instance, the mediator may contribute to a

---

[115] **BD**: In most traditional texts these are identified as royal legates and ambassadors, which perform similar functions.

profitable transaction and may help the querent earn or save money.

"Shall I inherit from my father?"

If the question is related to an inheritance from the father, or profit due to a business with the father, the lord of the 4th (the significator of the father) and the lord of the 5th (profit expected from the father) are considered. The lord of the Ascendant represents the querent, as always. Planets in the 5th house are related to the profit or inheritance expected from the father. The benefics, the Lot of Fortune, or the North Node being in the 5th indicates the querent will make a profit through his father.

Positive aspects or reception between the lord of the 2nd and the lord of the 5th, or the lord of the 2nd placed in the 5th and in positive aspect, also means the querent will make a profit through his father. Similarly, if the lord of the Ascendant or the lord of the 2nd is applying to a conjunction or a positive aspect with the Lot of Fortune, or applying to a conjunction with the North Node, the querent will take advantage of his father's wealth, or profit through a business with his father. If the lord of the 5th is burned, retrograde, or in a conjunction, square, or opposition with the malefics, or applying to a conjunction with the South Node, the querent will not get financial support from his father.

A conjunction or positive aspect between the lord of the 2nd with Venus or Jupiter, Jupiter being in the 2nd or in positive aspects or conjunction with the lord of the 2nd, indicates the querent will be able to get the financial support he wanted from his father.

If there is no applying aspect between the lord of the Ascendant and the lord of the 4th or 5th houses, but the Moon is transferring the light between these significators, or a slower third planet collects their light, the querent's expectation will come true and he will be able to get financial support from his father.

Any malefics (Saturn, Mars, and the South Node) in the 4th house may indicate that the querent's expectation from his father will not be realized. If the lord of the 5th is in a negative placement and in hard aspects, the father's financial situation is inadequate and the querent will not seize the opportunities he wanted. This problem is more significant when these malefics in the 4th or ruling the 4th are in negative aspects or a conjunction with the lord of the Ascendant or the Moon.

The same criteria are valid for questions related to questions on profits from real estate. As the 5th house is the 2nd from the 4th, it also represents profit from real estate.

QUESTIONS ON 6TH HOUSE MATTERS

This section pertains to questions related to diseases and weaknesses.

To answer such questions, the Ascendant, planets in the 1st house, the lord of the Ascendant, planets in the 6th, the lord of the 6th, and the Moon should be considered. The planet to which the Moon made her last aspect gives information about the disease, and the planet the Moon will next aspect gives information on the course of the disease.

William Lilly uses the houses as they map onto certain body parts, from the first house (head) to the twelfth (feet). For instance, he says: "If the first house be afflicted by the presence of an evil Planet and he Retrograde, Combust, Peregrine, slow in motion, or in square or opposition to any Planet who is Lord of the fourth, sixth, eighth or twelfth, the Disease is then in the Head, or in that or those parts of the Body which the Planet or Planets signify in that Sign then ascending. As if the Sign ascending be Cancer, and Saturn therein, you may judge, the sick party is afflicted in the Head, or such diseases as are incident to the Head, because that first house signifies in man's Body the Head, and is now afflicted by the position of Saturn in that house."[116]

Afterwards, he considers the sign where this malefic planet is and maps them onto the body in a way that derives from the signs they rule. Again using Saturn in Cancer, he says "you shall also judge the sick party is Diseased with a Looseness or Flux in the Belly, or an imperfection in the Reins[117] or Secrets,[118] or troubled with cold, raw Matter in his Stomach, because Saturn in Cancer does signify those members,[119] or else with some rotten Cough."[120]

Below you may see Lilly's reference table which helps explain his method. Saturn is the lord of Capricorn, so we can treat Capricorn as the head, all the way around to the twelfth sign from it (Sagittarius) indicating the feet—this is when *Saturn* is in these signs. (Other planets have their own derived signs.) When we count forward from Capricorn to Cancer, we move seven signs forward. Both the seventh house (in the house method) and Saturn's position in the seventh sign from Capricorn (in the sign method) indicate the same parts of the body. In the natural zodiac starting with Aries, the seventh sign is Libra, and consequently we understand why Saturn's position in the seventh sign from Capricorn likewise indicates the kidneys, belly and genitals. Saturn also rules Aquarius, so when we start with Aquarius and reach Cancer, we move six signs forward. The sixth natural sign is Virgo, which rules the intestines.

---

[116] Lilly, pp. 243-44.
[117] **BD**: That is, the kidneys.
[118] **BD**: That is, the genitals.
[119] **BD**: That is, "limbs" or organs of the body.
[120] Lilly, p. 244.

	♄	♃	♂	☉	♀	☿	☽
♈	Breast Arm	Neck Throat Heart Belly	Belly Head	Thighs	Kidneys Feet	Genitals Legs	Knees Head
♉	Heart Breast	Shoulder Arms Belly Neck	Kidneys Throat	Knees	Genitals Head	Thighs Feet	Legs Throat
♊	Belly Heart	Breast Kidneys Genitals	Genitals Arms Breast	Legs Ankles	Thighs Throat	Knees Head	Feet Shoulder Arms Thighs
♋	Kidneys Belly Genitals	Heart Genitals Thighs	Thighs	Knees	Knees Shoulders Arms	Legs Throat Arms	Head Breast Stomach
♌	Genitals Kidneys	Belly Thighs Knees	Knees Heart Belly	Head	Legs Breast, Heart	Feet Arms Shoulders Throat	Throat Stomach Heart
♍	Thighs Genitals Feet	Kidneys Knees	Legs belly	Throat	Feet Stomach Heart Belly	Head Breast Heart	Arms Shoulders Bowels
♎	Knees Thighs	Genitals Legs Head Eyes	Feet Kidneys Genitals	Shoulders Arms	Head Small intestines	Throat Heart Stomach Belly	Breast Kidneys Heart Belly
♏	Knees Legs	Thighs Feet	Head Genitals Arms Thighs	Breast Heart	Throat Kidneys Genitals	Shoulder Arms Bowels Back	Stomach Heart Genitals Belly
♐	Legs Feet	Knees Head Thighs	Throat Thighs Hands Feet	Heart Belly	Shoulders Arms Genitals Thighs	Breast Kidneys Heart Genitals	Bowels Thighs Back

	♄	♃	♂	☉	♀	☿	☽
♑	Head Feet	Legs Neck Eyes Knees	Arms Shoulders Knees Legs	Belly Back	Breast Heart Thighs	Stomach Heart Genitals	Kidneys Knees Thighs
♒	Neck Head	Feet Arms Shoulders Breast	Breast Legs Heart	Kidneys Genitals	Heart Knees	Bowels Thighs Heart	Genitals Legs Ankles
♓	Arms Shoulders Neck	Head Breast Heart	Heart Feet Belly Ankles	Genitals Thighs	Belly Legs Neck Throat	Kidneys Knees Genitals Thighs	Thighs Knees

Figure 14: Table of body parts, by planets in signs

I should admit that I personally do not use this method. I make my comments based on the body parts which are represented by the natural signs that the significators of illness are placed in. For instance, if Cancer is on the cusp of the 6th house, I judge that the querent may have health problems related to his stomach, breasts or lungs (the natural rulership of Cancer). If Saturn is in this house, I again think that the querent may have health problems related to his stomach, breasts or lungs, but because Saturn is there, I would warn the querent about possible risks related to those body parts because of his malefic presence. The sign where the Moon is placed also gives us valuable hints on the body parts that may be exposed to health problems.

In general, planets in the 6th and where the lord of the 6th is placed should be considered. The sign on the cusp of the 6th gives information on the type and nature of the disease. If there is any planet in the 6th house, the body parts represented by this planet may get damaged. The planet to which the lord of the 6th has made its most recent aspect, and the planet it is applying to, should be considered. The sign and the house the Moon is in, the planet to which the Moon made her most recent aspect, and the planet she approaches next, should also be considered. And of course, the nature of the aspect is also important! Consequently, it is possible to understand which part of the querent's body is exposed to an illness, its nature and quality, and the course of illness.

The majority of the significators placed in fiery signs represent inflammatory diseases; in earthy signs, illnesses caused by toxic substances; in airy signs, diseases related to the nervous and respiratory system, intestinal gas, spasms, anxiety, insomnia; in watery signs, diseases caused by emotional stress, phlegm, and discharge.

The quality of the signs where the significators are placed should also be considered. If the majority of the significators are in cardinal signs, the illness is an acute one. Cardinal signs represent positive or negative quick developments. If the majority are in fixed signs, the illness may last long and even get chronic. If the majority are in mutable signs, the course of the illness may change, or the illness may recur.

Saturn represents chronic diseases and Mars represents acute diseases. According to Lilly, "hot and dry Diseases, which are procreated from the influence of Mars and the Sun are but short, and are determined by the motion of the Moon: Saturn produces chronic Infirmities; Jupiter and Sun short; Mars more short, violent and quick; Venus a mean between both; Mercury divers and inconstant; the Moon such as do again revert, as the Falling-sickness, Giddiness, Swimming of the head, Gouts, &c."[121]

If the last degrees of a sign are on the cusp of the 6th, or if the lord of the 6th or the Moon is placed in the last degrees of a sign, the illness is about to end, or is about to proceed to another phase. The prediction should be made by considering whether that planet is comfortable in the sign it will move to. A planet in the last de-

---

[121] Lilly, pp. 247-248.

grees of a house towards the beginning of the next house requires a similar interpretation. To understand when this change will take place, we should consider how many degrees are needed to change, and apply our symbolic methods. If the planet enters a cardinal sign, the course of the illness changes within a shorter period of time (days, weeks); if it enters a mutable sign the change occurs in the medium term (weeks, months); if a fixed sign, over the long term (months, years).

If the lord of the 6th is placed in one of the malefic houses (6th, 8th, 12th) and has negative aspects with the other planets, especially with the lords of the 6th, 8th, or 12th houses or with the malefics, if it is burned or entering into burning, if the Moon also has negative aspects—all of these indicators show that the illness is a bad one or will get worse. If the lord of the 6th is retrograde, the illness recurs or its course changes.

If one of the benefics is in the 6th or the lord of the 6th house is in positive aspects with the benefics, the querent recovers. The application of the lord of the 6th to a conjunction, sextile, or trine with Jupiter is a positive situation. An application to a conjunction, sextile, or trine with Venus, or conjunction with the North Node, also indicates a positive development.

If one of the malefics is in the 6th, the illness gets problematic. The querent should take this illness seriously. The application of the lord of the 6th to a conjunction, square, or opposition with the malefics, or to a conjunction with the South Node or conjunction with the Sun indicates that the illness develops in a negative way, or the querent should fight the illness.

When the positions of the lord of the Ascendant and the lord of the 6th are compared, if the lord of the 6th is stronger than the other, the disease may progress. On the other hand, if the lord of the Ascendant is stronger than the lord of the 6th, the patient may get well, even if he does not get medical support. If the lord of the Ascendant is stronger than the lord of the 8th, then life overcomes death. If the contrary is true, then death is likely. Only one criterion is not enough for predicting death, but this is one of the main indicators.

If the lord of the 6th is retrograde or slow moving, the disease may last for a long time. The lord of the 6th in the 12th suggests the disease will last or become chronic, especially if this lord is in one of the fixed signs and in an applying aspect to Saturn. The lord of the 6th in the 8th makes us think the disease will result in death, especially if this significator in the 8th is in hard aspects with the malefics or applying to a conjunction with the Sun. The lord of the 8th in the 6th represents the same thing.

The lord of the 1st house placed in the 6th indicates the querent does things that make him sick; the lord of the 6th in the 1st shows that the querent may already have the disease. If the lord of the 6th is a malefic and is in a negative aspect with the lord of the Ascendant, the disease may become dangerous.

Even if the other significators in a horary chart are in negative placements, if the lord of the Ascendant in a strong position it is a positive indicator that the querent will get healthy. Even if the lord of the Ascendant is in the 8th, if it is not in detriment and there are applying aspects with the benefics and strong planets, the querent will get healthy. However, when the lord of the Ascendant is in the 8th or 4th (which represent the end of life), in detriment or fall, and applying to a conjunction with the Sun, the querent faces serious risks.

Negative aspects between the lord of the Ascendant and the lords of the 6th, 8th, or 12th houses, lead us to think that the querent's illness will progress in a negative way. However, this alone cannot be a definitive criterion. The Moon or the lord of the 6th in negative aspects with the lords of these houses, or with the malefics, should also be considered. The lord of the Ascendant placed in a weak sign or house, indicates the querent is tired, weak, or anxious and unable to manage the condition.

If the lord of the Ascendant, the lord of the 6th, or the Moon is burned (that is, when the significator is entering into burning), the disease shows a negative progress. For planets slower than the Sun (Mars, Jupiter, Saturn), this occurs when the Sun is applying to conjunction with them; for the fast moving planets (the Moon, Mercury, Venus), this is when they apply to him. If the Moon is waning or applying to a conjunction with the South Node or the Sun, the querent's disease will show a negative progress.

The luminaries being weakly placed, under the horizon, or in negative aspects with the malefics, indicate that the querent's health is in a weak position because the Moon represents the body and health, and the Sun represents the life force.

Even if the luminaries are in negative aspects with the malefics, so long as they are supported by the benefics the course of the disease may progress positively. The Sun applying to a harmonious aspect with Jupiter is also an indication that the querent will get better.

Benefics being more strongly placed as compared with the malefics, also shows that the querent's health will improve.

If the Moon and Ascendant are not negatively aspected but their lords are in negative aspects, the health problem is not physical but a spiritual one.

The aspects of the Moon are crucial factors in determining the course of the disease. If the Moon is separating from a conjunction, square, or opposition with one of the malefics and applying to a conjunction, square, or opposition with a malefic, the querent's health will get worse. On the other hand, if the Moon is separating from a conjunction, sextile, or trine with a benefic and applying to a conjunction, sextile, or trine with a benefic, the querent's health will get better.

If the Moon has good aspects and the lord of the Ascendant is not afflicted, there is not much to worry about regarding the disease. The Moon transferring the light of the lord of the Ascendant to the lord of the 6th through a negative aspect indicates that the querent will become sick; the Moon transferring the light of the lord of the Ascendant to the lord of the 8th shows the querent will be faced with a fatal risk or will have surgery. However, all other factors should be considered and the question should not be answered based on only one criterion.

If there is no negative aspect between the lord of the Ascendant and the lord of the 8th but there is a harmonious aspect or mutual reception between them, the risk of death is low. The querent overcomes the disease even if he experiences difficulties during the course of the disease.

The lord of the Ascendant, the Moon, or the lord of the 8th in conjunction with a malefic fixed star such as Algol, indicates fatal diseases, if confirmed by other significators.

The 7th house should be considered for questions relating to the doctor who treats the disease. If the lord of the 7th is in detriment or badly placed, the doctor may not be successful in healing the patient.

The 10th house should be considered to see if the treatment of the disease will be successful or not. If the benefics are in the 10th, or if the lord of the 10th is in a strong position and supported by the benefics, the querent will benefit from the treatment. If the malefics are in the 10th or if the lord of the 10th is ill-placed, or if it is detriment, the querent will not benefit from the treatment.

If the significators are not favorable, the querent may suffer.

The 4th house should be considered for the result of the treatment. If malefics are in the 4th or there is an inharmonious aspect between the lord of the 4th and the lord of the 8th, the treatment does not bring the expected results and, if confirmed by the other significators, death may be the result.

QUESTIONS ON 7TH HOUSE MATTERS

Under this heading I give practical advice on questions related to marriage and partnerships.

Marriage and relationships

The Ascendant, planets in it, and its lord represent the querent, while the 7th, planets in it, and its lord represent the quaesited. If there are harmonious aspects between these significators at the time of the question, then a positive result is expected. If there is no aspect between them but the Moon is transferring the light to a conjunction or harmonious aspect between them, or a third planet slower than them is collecting their light, the result is positive. If the aspect is a negative one but there is mutual reception between the significators, then even though a negative outcome is expected, a positive outcome may be welcomed after having some problems. If the main significators related to the marriage or relationship do not aspect each other and a third planet is collecting or transferring the light, the problem is solved by the help of third parties.

The Sun is the main significator for the man and Venus is the main significator for the woman. If there is an approaching conjunction between them, the question is answered positively. When there is a conjunction between the Sun and Venus, a burned Venus is not interpreted as a problem, but the querent and the quaesited meet and a positive outcome is expected. If the querent is a woman, the Sun's position should be considered for the quaesited, and if the querent is a man the position of Venus should be considered for the quaesited. (Venus is the significator and not the Moon, because the Moon represents the general course of events.)

The Moon approaching a conjunction or harmonious aspect with Venus means the outcome is positive, whether the querent is a woman or man.

The Sun or Venus ruling the 1st or 7th houses alters the situation, as these planets are then the significators of those specific houses. To explain: if Leo is rising at the time of the question and the querent is a woman, the Sun becomes the significator of the woman who asks the question.

If the question is about the relationship between a man and another man, or with a woman and another woman, then the Sun and Venus cannot be used in this method.

While answering questions about marriage and relationships, if the significator of the querent is strong, the querent has power. If the significator is weak, the querent has limited power to manage the issue and feels anxious.

The lord of the 7th placed in the 1st indicates there will be a relationship between the querent and the quaesited. The lord of the 1st house in the 7th house is a positive significator, but does not confirm that a relationship will start unless other significators also support this. If the lord of the Ascendant is in the 7th or is in a harmonious aspect or conjunction with the lord of the 7th, the relationship is confirmed. If the lord of the Ascendant in the 7th makes an aspect with the Moon, and the Moon transfers its light to the lord of the 7th, again the relationship is confirmed.

If there is no aspect between the lord of the Ascendant and the lord of the 7th, nor does the Moon transfer light, and no third planet collects the light, we should see whether or not there is mutual reception between these planets. If there is no reception, an antiscion should be considered. If there is an antiscion between these two planets, the marriage or a relationship is likely. If there is a contra-antiscion, there will not be a marriage nor a relationship.

Even if there is a negative aspect between the lord of the Ascendant and the lord of the 7th, if there is a mutual reception between them then a marriage or relationship may start.

The lord of the 7th house in the 1st indicates the quaesited is interested in the querent. The lord of the 1st house in the 7th shows the querent is interested in the quaesited. On the other hand, if the lord of the 7th is in the 7th, the quaesited is only interested in himself, not in the querent. This means that in terms of making a proposal the querent may not get a positive answer. If the lord of the 1st is in the 1st, the querent is not interested in the other party despite being the one asking the question.

The house where the lord of the 1st and/or the Moon is placed shows what the querent is asking for. If the lord of the 1st or the Moon is in the 8th, the querent is interested in the financial conditions of the quaesited. If the lord of the Ascendant or the Moon is in the 5th, the querent is rather interested in sexuality.

If there is no aspect, reception, or antiscion between the significators of the querent and quaesited, if the Moon is not transferring the light between these significators, nor does another planet collect the light, nor is there a planet at the cusp of the 7th confirming the marriage, there will not be a relationship or marriage.

When the lord of the Ascendant applies to an aspect with the lord of the 7th, if one of them shifts to another sign before the aspect becomes exact, the conditions of these people will change before the marriage or relationship starts, and they will change their directions.

As the lord of the Ascendant applies to a conjunction or positive aspect with the lord of the 7th, if one of them makes an aspect with another planet before their own aspect becomes exact, then a third person will interfere and the course of the relationship will change. The house ruled by this interfering planet represents the person or the matter that interferes. For instance, if this interfering planet is the lord of the 3rd, the problem stems from the siblings or one's close circle. If it is the lord of the 2nd or 8th, the problem is related to money. By predicting the reason for this intervention, we may consider the ways to avoid possible problems in the course of events. If the interfering planet makes positive aspects with the main significators, then this person or event may have a positive influence on the relationship. By being aware of this support, it may be possible to take more advantage of the situation.

Positive indicators of marriage in a horary chart are: malefics not being in the 7th house, the lord of the 7th house not being retrograde or burned, and Venus (the general significator for marriage) not being in detriment.

A Moon-Sun square or opposition indicates problems in marriage and relationships, but this alone does not indicate divorce or separation.

If the querent is a woman and the Sun is afflicted in some way, applying to a conjunction or negative aspect with the malefics, the querent experiences problems with the quaesited man. This man may have some troubles and barriers. If the querent is a man and Venus is afflicted, applying to a conjunction or negative aspects with the malefics, the querent experiences problems with the quaesited woman. This woman may have some troubles and barriers. In such questions, not the Moon, but Venus, indicates the woman (as the Moon represents the course of the events).

If there is a planet in the 7th of the horary chart, the nature of this planet gives information about the quaesited. For instance, if Mercury is in the 7th the quaesited is a communicative, talkative, smart, and skillful person. Venus in the 7th indicates the quaesited is pretty, beautiful, harmonious, easygoing, and skilled in arts. If Jupiter is in the 7th, the quaesited is religious, literate, cultured, rich, or a foreigner, or someone who has a connection with foreign countries.

For questions on marriage, we should consider the following: if there is an opposition between the two significators, if the significators are about to change signs, and whether they are retrograde or direct. If two significators are in opposition but there is reception between them, the difficulty of the relationship may lessen but does not disappear. A square with reception may lessen the difficulties. But an opposition (even with a reception), means the marriage may not take place.

The lord of the 7th house leaving the 1st house and moving towards the 2nd or, leaving the sign on the cusp of the 1st house, or leaving the sign of the Lot of marriage (see below), may show the spouse is about to leave the querent, or the conditions of the spouse are about to change.

Here is another scenario which uses dignities. Suppose that the querent is a man and the lord of the 7th is in one of the signs it rules (showing that the woman is focused on herself and secure in her current situation), while the Sun (indicating the querent or man) is in the sign where the lord of the 7th house is in detriment. In this tough situation, there will probably not be a love affair between the two without some other powerful indications, because the planets do not show a positive relationship to the dignities of the other person: the significator of the woman is in her own dignity and the Sun is in a place where the lord of the 7th is uncomfortable.

Or, let the Moon be in a mute sign and the lord of the 7th is in its own dignity: the other person will be focused on him- or herself, rather than the querent (due to being in its own dignity). In this case, unless the querent speaks up (since the Moon suggests keeping silent), the relationship will not work.

The timing of marriage

Count the number of degrees up to the point when the aspect between the lord of the Ascendant and the lord of the 7th will be exact, or when the Moon reaches the exact degree while transferring the light, or when the collection of light will reach the exact degree, or when a planet applies to the cusp of the 7th. When the exactness of the aspect or conjunction is in a cardinal sign, it indicates the querent will marry in the short term; in mutable signs, in the middle term; in fixed signs, over the long term. Cardinal signs indicate days, mutable signs indicate months, and fixed signs indicate years. Fast significators also speed up the time.

"Who stirs up the problem?"

For this question, the Ascendant and its lord, and the 7th and its lord, should be considered. To understand who stirs up the problem, the most recent aspects of the significators should be observed, as the issue already stems from the past.

If the lord of the Ascendant makes negative aspects, the problems stem from the querent; the same is true for malefics (Saturn, Mars, the South Node) in the 1st. If the lord of the 7th makes negative aspects, the problems stem from the quaesited; the same is true for malefics placed in the 7th.

If the lord of the 7th is in the 12th and its recent aspects are negative, separating from the malefics, then we may conclude that the deceiving party in this relationship is the quaesited. On the other hand, if the lord of the Ascendant is in the twelfth house and its recent aspects are negative, separating from the malefics, the querent may be the one who deceives.

As the lord of the Ascendant represents the querent and the lord of the 7th represents the quaesited, we look to which of those significators is in a fixed sign, and the quality of the sign where Venus is placed—if the querent is a man asking a question about the woman's loyalty. (If the querent is a woman, we look at the sign and quality of the sign which the Sun is in.) Significators in fixed signs are considered as an indicator of loyalty by the ancient astrologers. On the other hand, this cannot be a sole indicator and other factors should be examined. For questions about adultery, a conjunction or negative aspect with Mars is considered; even so, this again is not a sole indicator. William Lilly emphasizes that astrology requires making judgments on questions, but it is better to remain silent in certain types of questions because any unfortunate statement may cause unpleasant things.[122]

In the case of an unhappy marriage or relationship, the previous aspects of the Sun and Venus are considered in order to understand who is more affected in this situation. If the Sun's previous aspects are negative, the man is unhappy; if Venus, the woman is unhappy.

The lord of the Ascendant applying to a negative aspect, or malefics being in the 7th house, each shows that the querent will not be happy in a marriage or relationship. The lord of the 7th applying to negative aspects, or malefics being in the 7th, means the quaesited will not be happy.

If the lord of the Ascendant, the lord of the 7th, or the Moon is in the 12th house, then some secret, out-of-control, or beyond-control factors may prevail in the marriage or relationship. If all of the significators are in the 12th, the marriage or relationship will never work well, or it is unfavorable.

Questions about third parties

Many questions on relationships include other people! For instance, questions like "I am married but shall I have a future with my lover?" are common. The lord of the 7th house should always be considered for the quaesited. In such cases, Saturn may be considered for the unwanted husband. A planet which has just made an aspect with the querent's significators may be considered for the querent's lover. For instance, if this significator is a planet in the 10th then the lover may be someone from the business environment.

Let's assume that a woman asks "Shall my marriage survive?" and the lord of the 1st house is Venus: the lord of the 7th is therefore Mars, and the Sun represents the woman's husband. Let's

---

[122] Lilly, p. 313.

assume that both Mars and the Sun are in Cancer, and the Moon is in Pisces. All of these significators are in signs ruled by Jupiter. So, the things represented by Jupiter are important for all those parties. The Sun, who represents the husband, exalts Jupiter. That means the person represented by the Sun shows great respect (exaltation) to the person represented by Jupiter. Here, Jupiter may represent a known mistress of the husband.

According to John Frawley, the lords of the Ascendant and the 7th house, the Moon, the Sun, and Venus all represent different things. The lords of the 1st and 7th represent the individuality of the people involved; they are the "head." The Moon is the significator of the querent but especially represents the emotions of the querent; she is the "heart." The Sun or Venus is related to sexual attraction, passions and animal instincts.[123]

The lord of the 1st on the cusp of the 7th means it is in a sign where it is in detriment. This means that the querent loves the quaesited, but he is unguarded because of this love. The lord of the 1st placed in the other sign ruled by the lord of the 7th also represents the same thing. This situation can also suggest that the querent's love is linked to being unhappy and weak (i.e., in detriment), so that when the unhappiness of the querent dissolves, his love may also end. The same applies when the lord of the 7th is in the 1st or in the other sign ruled by the lord of the 1st.

In questions concerning relationships, if one of the main significators is in contact with another planet which is not a significator, we may conclude that another person is involved behind the scenes or is of interest to the querent or quaesited (such as another lover).

---

[123] Frawley, p. 193.

Lots of marriage and divorce

There are many natal Lots for marriage and relationships, but good ones for use in horary are the following:

Lot of marriage: Ascendant + DSC − Venus (from Venus to the Descendant, projected from the Ascendant)

Lot of Divorce:[124] Ascendant + DSC − Mars (from Mars to the Descendant, projected from the Ascendant)

Instead of looking at which house the Lot of marriage is in, consider the place of its lord. If the lord is in one of the fixed signs, the marriage will not end; if in one of the cardinal signs, the marriage will end due to taking quick action; and if in one of the mutable signs, the marriage will have ups and downs. If the lord of the Lot of marriage is in detriment, especially if it is in a conjunction or negative aspect with planets like Saturn and Uranus, there will be some difficulties in the marriage.

Mars and Uranus may be significators of divorce on their own, if they are in a conjunction, square, or opposition with the significators of marriage (such as the lord of the Lot of marriage, the lord of the 1st, or the lord of the 7th). If the question is "Will this relationship continue," Uranus on the cusp of the 7th tells us that the answer is "no."

The Lot of divorce and its lord in negative aspects with other planets, especially its conjunction or negative aspects with Mars, Saturn, or Uranus, show the divorce will be problematic.

---

[124] Frawley, p. 123.

QUESTIONS ON 8ᵀᴴ HOUSE MATTERS

These questions relate to threats and dangers, mutual earnings, and debts.

"Will he survive?"

First, we need to determine the relationship between the querent and the quaesited. The querent is represented by the lord of the 1st house. To determine the significator of the quaesited, we should count houses relative to the Ascendant. If the quaesited is the querent's sibling, the planets in the 3rd house and the lord of the 3rd are the significators of the quaesited. The Moon is also one of the significators of the quaesited, as well as being the significator of the course of the events.

As this question is related to death, we should consider the 8th house of the horary chart but also the 8th relative of the house of the quaesited. For instance, if the quaesited is the querent's sibling, we should start with the 3rd house (the sibling) and count 8 houses until we reach the 10th (the sibling's death). If malefics are placed in the 8th or in the derived 8th, or if the lord of that house is under pressure, then we may conclude that the quaesited has a risk of death. When such a question is asked, we may also consider the 4th house of the chart or the derived 4th from the quaesited (in the example of a sibling, this would be the 6th, which is the 4th from the 3rd).

If the significator of the quaesited or the Moon is in detriment, entering into burning, or in negative aspects with the lord of the 8th or the derived 8th, then the quaesited has a risk of death. If the Moon or the significator of the quaesited is separating from any negative aspect with the above-mentioned significator, we may conclude that the quaesited had a risk of death in the past but now the risk is about to decrease. However when negative aspects are applying, the risk of death increases.

If the question is about a missing person, then we should consider the place and future aspects of the lord of the quaesited and the Moon. If either significator is in one of the angular houses, in a strong position, without any applying negative aspects, we may conclude that the quaesited is alive and well. The house and the sign where this significator is, informs us as to where the quaesited may be. If this planet is in the 12th house, the quaesited may be in a closed and secluded place; if in the 3rd, he is nearby; if in the 9th or 7th, he is far away. If the significator is in a weak house position, we may conclude that the quaesited is also weak and cannot change the course of events. If the significator is in a strong position, the quaesited may take care of himself and change the conditions through his own choice. If the significator is in detriment or fall, the quaesited may be hurt or cannot manage any of the circumstances; he may be anxious, weak, or unhealthy. This is a strong possibility when the aspects of the planet and the Moon are negative. The house where this significator is, and the houses it rules, inform us as to who may harm the quaesited and what the conditions are.

If the lord of the quaesited is retrograde, or if the Moon conjoins with a retrograde planet, the quaesited returns suddenly and unexpectedly. If this retrograde planet is also in detriment or about to be in detriment, the quaesited returns in a hurt or damaged condition.

If the significator of the quaesited is in the last degrees of a sign and about to shift into the next sign, we may conclude that the conditions of the quaesited are about to change. If the significator is in its dignity and is shifting to the sign of its detriment or fall, the conditions of the quaesited will change negatively. If the significator is already in detriment, fall, or peregrine, and is shifting into its dignity, the conditions of the quaesited will change positively. For instance, if Venus is the significator of the quaesited and is in the last degree of Virgo, about to enter Libra, the condition of the quaesited changes in a positive direction. But if Venus is in the last degree of Libra and about to enter Scorpio, the conditions of the quaesited will change negatively. If the significator of the quaesited has just entered into a sign, the existing conditions have just changed.

"When?"

To predict the time of the change in the quaesited's condition, we should consider the number of degrees needed for the significator to change its sign, or make an exact aspect, or for the Moon to make her next exact aspect. There are two ways for converting these degrees into a time unit: we may convert them symbolically into time units as we have done before, or we may find the "real" time when they will occur, through an ephemeris or astrological software. If the applying aspect of the significator or the Moon is in angular houses, it will be realized in the short term; when in succedent houses, in the middle term; and when in the cadent houses, over the long term.

Profit through the spouse or a partner

The Ascendant, its lord, and planets in the 1st represent the querent; the lord of the 7th and planets in it represent the quaesited. Planets in the 8th house (the derived 2nd for the spouse or partner) and the lord of the 8th indicate if it is possible to make a profit through the quaesited.

Benefics (Jupiter, Venus, the Sun, North Node, and the Lot of Fortune) in the 8th house show that the quaesited will make a profit through the quaesited (whether spouse, partner, or others). On the other hand, malefics (Saturn, Mars, the South Node) placed in the 8th indicate that the querent will not make money through the quaesited. The positions of the malefics (Saturn and Mars) should also be considered: if they are in their dignities, we may conclude that the querent will obtain the money only after some effort.

If the planets in the 8th or the lord of the 8th are retrograde, then making money takes some time; some difficulties may arise. If the lord of the 8th is quick in motion, then profit is made quickly. Even if the significators are benefics, if they are retrograde, burned, or are applying to negative aspects with the malefics, we may conclude that the profit will not be obtained easily: some difficulties and delays will be experienced.

If the lord of the 8th is applying to a conjunction or aspect with the Lot of Fortune, and is not afflicted by the malefics, it indicates a good profit. If the lord of the Lot of Fortune is in a good position, it strengthens this possibility.

The lord of the 8th being in the 8th, 1st, or 2nd house indicates the querent will get money as a result of an inheritance or common profit. The lord of the 8th being in conjunction, sextile, or trine with the lord of the 2nd clinches this judgment.

If the significators are in square or opposition but also in reception, then profit is made after some difficulties, or after much effort. On the other hand, the significator of the querent being in the 8th does not ensure profit if it has no good aspects with the lord of the 2nd or the Moon.

If the South Node is in the 8th, the querent cannot get the expected money. It is possible that the querent may be deceived or cheated in financial issues with the partners. This would be further confirmed by an afflicted lord of the 7th and/or 8th houses.

Questions related to threats

The Ascendant, the lord of the Ascendant, and the Moon are the significators of the querent. If the querent knows the person who threatens, the quaesited is represented by the 7th and its lord. If the querent does not know who the quaesited is, then he is represented by the 12th house and its lord.

If malefics (Saturn, Mars, the South Node) are placed in the 1st house, it shows the threat is true and the querent will be hurt somehow. If the querent knows the person who threatens him, then a negative aspect between the lords of the 1st and 7th houses indicates that the querent and the quaesited will have problems. If these two significators are applying to conjunction, a confrontation may follow. If the querent does not know the person who threatens him, then a negative aspect between the lords of the 1st and 12th houses shows that the querent and the quaesited will have problems. If these two significators are applying by conjunction, a confrontation may follow.

If the lord of the Ascendant or the Moon is applying to an aspect with the benefics, the threat will not bring a negative result. If the lord of the Ascendant or the Moon is applying to a conjunction or negative aspect, the threat may bring an unwanted result. If the lord of the Ascendant or the Moon is applying to a negative aspect with the lord of the 8th or 12th houses, the querent may be harmed, especially if these houses are ruled by malefics.

The 12th house is related to fears, anxieties, and secret enemies. If the lord of the 12th is in a strong position and applying to a negative aspect with the significator of the quaesited, we may conclude that the querent's enemy is strong and may harm him. If the lord of the 12th is in the 12th, the quaesited is about to betray the querent. If this planet is about to enter the 1st house, the hidden enemy will show up soon.

If the querent wants to know who that hidden enemy is, the house where the lord of the 12th house is, or the house ruled by a planet in the 12th, should be considered. For instance, if the lord of the 12th is in the 11th or if the planet in the 12th rules the 11th, the secret enemy is someone from the social environment of the querent. If the significator in the 12th is the lord of the 10th, the secret enemy is someone from the business environment, or someone in a managerial position.

For such questions we should also consider whether the lord of the Ascendant and the significator of the one who threatens the querent (the lord of the 7th or 12th) are applying to each other. If they are applying by a positive aspect, the threat does not work or the parties will make a compromise. If these significators apply by a negative aspect, the parties are in disagreement and have problems.

If the lord of the Ascendant is applying to an aspect with the malefics, the querent will get into trouble. The lord of the Ascendant applying to a conjunction or a negative aspect with Mars brings violence and fights, with Saturn it brings restrictions and sabotage, and with the South Node it brings disgrace.

If there is no major aspect between the lord of the Ascendant and the significator of the threatening person (the lord of the 7th or 12th) but the Moon is transferring the light or a slow moving planet is collecting the light of these two, then someone will intervene. If the collection or transfer of light occurs through negative aspects, the mediators will be harmful. If the collection or transfer of light occurs through positive aspects, the mediators will be beneficial.

According to William Lilly, if the Moon is in the 6th, 8th, or 12th houses and applying to a planet in a cadent house, there is no need to worry; even if the news of a threat will be effective for a long period of time, everything will take shape and problems will disappear. A Moon-Sun trine solves the problems suddenly.[125]

Borrowing and lending money

The querent is represented by the Ascendant, the lord of the Ascendant, and the Moon. The 2nd house, its lord, and the planets in it represent the querent's budget and resources. The 8th house, its lord, and the planets in it represent the money borrowed, or the credit.

---

[125] Lilly, p. 414.

If the significator of the querent (the lord of the Ascendant) or the Moon is applying to a conjunction or a positive aspect with the lord of the 7th or planets in the 7th, we may conclude that the querent will have a good meeting with the person or institution from whom he requested the money. If the lord of the Ascendant or the Moon is in a harmonious aspect with the lord of the 8th, the querent gets the loan he asked for. If at the same time the lord of the 2nd is in a strong position, the querent does not have any problems paying back his loan. An applying positive aspect between the lord of the 2nd and the lord of the 8th strengthens this judgment. On the other hand, if there is an applying negative aspect between the lord of the 2nd and the lord of the 8th, and if the Moon is applying to a negative aspect, we should not recommend that the querent borrow money because he may possibly have problems in repayment.

The same method is used for questions related to joint resources, allowance, compensations, insurance payments, and taxes, as they are also related to the 8th house. The aspects between the lord of the Ascendant or the Moon and the lord of the 7th should be considered. If the applying aspects are positive, starting joint efforts with a partner or spouse is recommended; if the applying aspects are negative, a partnership is not recommended as problems would be likely. Negative aspects between the lord of the 2nd and the lord of the 8th indicate problems related to repayment. If the lord of the 8th is applying to a negative aspect, the collection of debts and joint resources will be problematic.

QUESTIONS ON 9ᵀᴴ HOUSE MATTERS

Topics here relate to long-distance travel, educational issues, and exams.

Long-distance travel

The 9th house should be considered for questions concerning long distance travel. Planets in the 9th and the lord of the 9th are the main significators. If any of the benefics (Jupiter, Venus, the North Node, and the Lot of Fortune) are placed in the 9th, or if the lord of the 9th is well placed, the querent will benefit from that journey. If any malefic (Saturn, Mars, and the South Node) is placed in this house or if the lord of the 9th is afflicted, the querent will not get what he expected from this journey, or he may even receive harm.

The querent is again represented by the planet in the Ascendant and the lord of the Ascendant. The aspects between the lord of the Ascendant or the Moon and the lord of the 9th house/or the planets in the 9th house should be considered. If there is no aspect between them, then a collection or transfer of the light is considered. Should there be an inharmonious aspect between the lord of the Ascendant and the lord of the 9th, but they are in mutual reception, the possible difficulties and obstacles would be overcome and the querent would get a positive result. If there is no aspect nor mutual reception between the lord of the Ascendant and the lord of the 9th, then any antiscion or contra-antiscion should be considered. In the case of an antiscion between the significators, the querent will have a good journey; however if there is a contra-antiscion, the querent will not have a good journey.

If the question is related to a business trip, the lord of the 10th house and planets in it should be considered. If the lord of the 10th is in the 10th, or applying to a harmonious aspect with the lord of the 9th and/or the lord of the Ascendant, the querent will have a nice trip which is beneficial for his business: since the 10th is the

2nd from the 9th (by derived houses), the querent will earn money from this trip. If there is a positive aspect between the lord of the 2nd and the lord of the 10th, or if the Moon is transferring the light between them, or another planet is collecting their light, the prediction of financial gain that the querent is about to get from the journey, is strengthened. On the other hand, if there are negative aspects and no mutual reception, the querent cannot generate the income that he expected from the journey.

As the 8th house is related to the possibility of earning or getting money from another person, it should also be considered for questions related to business trips with an expectation of generating income. If malefics are placed in the 8th, or if the lord of the 8th is afflicted, if there are negative aspects between the lord of the 8th and the lord of the Ascendant or the Moon, the querent may lose money due to the journey. On the other hand, if any of the benefics are placed in the 8th, or if the lord of the 8th is in a conjunction or positive aspect with the benefics, the lord of the Ascendant, or the Moon, the querent will generate profit through the business trip.

The house where the lord of the Ascendant is located should be considered. For instance, if the lord of the Ascendant is in the 6th and in negative aspect with the lord of the 9th, the querent may delay his trip due to his health problems, or he may get sick during his journey. If the lord of the Ascendant is in the 12th and in negative aspect with the lord of the 9th, the querent may experience some problems or losses during his journey due to reasons beyond his control, or some people may try to restrict him through behind-the-scenes activities. The lord of the Ascendant or the Moon entering into burning is also a negative situation. Consider the house where the burned planet is, and from it the reason for that possible negativity may be predicted.

If the one taking the journey is not the querent, we should carefully determine the house which will represent this person. If the querent asks "How will my son's trip be or go?" then the 1st house (which is the 9th house from the 5th) should be considered. Here, the significators are the lord of the 5th house (the child), the lord of the 1st house (his or her journey), and the Moon. In such questions, the Moon represents the general course of the events. If the querent asks "How will my sibling's trip be?" then the 11th house (the 9th house from the 3rd) should be considered. Here, the significators are the lord of the 3rd (the sibling), the lord of the 11th (his or her journey), and the Moon. The planets in those related houses also inform us as to the course of the events. For instance, in a question about the spouse's trip and any profit from it, if a benefic (Jupiter, Venus, North Node, or the Lot of Fortune) is placed in the 7th house (spouse), in the 3rd house (the 9th from the 7th, his or her journey), or in the 4th house (the 10th house from the 7th, business success from that journey), the judgment will be positive. Of course, the position of the lord of the Ascendant should be considered, as it is in all types of questions.

If one of the significators is in the last degrees of any sign and about to change signs, the conditions are likely to change. In such a situation we should consider how the power of that planet changes while shifting to another sign. If the significator is shifting to a sign where it is powerful, then positive developments may be expected from the trip. If this significator is the lord of the 9th and about to shift to a sign where it is more powerful, then positive developments may be expected. If the lord of the Ascendant is shifting into a sign where it is weaker, the querent's conditions will change for the worse. If the Moon is changing signs, the course of the events may change.

The timing of the journey

When the question is about the timing of a journey, the speed of the main significators, whether they are retrograde or direct, placed in cardinal-fixed-mutable signs, and the houses they are placed in, should be considered. The main significators here are the rising sign, planets in the 1st, the lord of the Ascendant, the Moon, planets in the 9th, and the lord of the 9th.

If the most of the significators are direct and quick in motion, the journey will be quick. If some of the significators are retrograde or slow in motion, the journey may be delayed.

Most of the significators being placed in cardinal signs indicates that the querent will take the journey within a short time; in the mutable signs, in the middle term; in fixed signs, over the long term. The quality of the sign on the cusp of the 9th may also be considered. A fixed sign at the cusp of the 9th indicates that the journey will start after a long time, whereas a mutable sign indicates some changes to the journey may occur. If the most of the significators are placed in mutable signs, then some changes related to the journey may occur, or the querent may change his mind. The Moon and/or Mercury placed in mutable signs also supports this prediction.

Most of the significators placed in angular houses give a start to the journey in the short term; in succedent houses, in the middle term; in cadent houses, over the long term. If the significators promise a journey, the chart is radical.

The most important point that should be considered for the timing of a journey is the degree when the aspects will be exact. For instance, if there are 3° for the lord of the Ascendant or the Moon to make an exact trine with the lord of the 9th, the journey will start after 3 units of time. This unit is determined by the qualities of the sign where the significators are placed (cardinal, fixed, mutable), and the houses they are in (see above).

The lord of the 9th placed in the 1st represents the possibility of a journey, and also within a short period of time. The lord of the 1st placed in the 9th does not assure a journey: an aspect between the lord of the Ascendant and the lord of the 9th, a transfer of light between them, or a mutual reception or antiscion, is needed.

If the querent is asking a question about a journey which was taken in the past, the separating aspects of the lord of the Ascendant or the lord of the related house, and the Moon, should be considered. The planet which the significator of the querent last aspected is used for making a judgment about the recent past of the querent. The planet to which the significator will apply, shows what the querent will meet in the future.

If the querent is waiting for news from someone, he may get this news within a short time if the Moon or Mercury is in the 1st house at the time of the question. The degrees between those planets and the degree of the Ascendant shows the units of time after which the news will arrive. The above-mentioned rules are valid for determining the time. Lilly states, "If you would know whether the News or Letters which are to come be good or ill, look from whom Mercury and the Moon are separate; if the separation be from a *Fortune*, it notes good news, and joyful; but if from ill *Fortunes*, judge the contrary."[126]

Education and exams

Here the planets in the Ascendant, the lord of the Ascendant, and the Moon are the significators of the querent. The significator of the quaesited is determined by deriving houses from the Ascendant, as before. If the querent is asking about his children, the planets in the 5th, the lord of the 5th, and the Moon are the significator of the querent's children, while planets in the 1st and the lord of the 1st (the 9th house from the 5th) represent their higher education; the 2nd house (the 10th from the 5th) indicates their success.

If the querent is asking for himself, and the benefics (Jupiter, Venus, the North Node, and the Lot of Fortune) are placed in the Ascendant or in the 9th or 10th houses, the querent passes the exam. The lord of the Ascendant in positive aspects with the lord of

---

[126] Lilly, p. 428.

the 9th and/or 10th houses, or the Moon transferring the light between these significators, or the Moon's positive aspects with the lords of the 9th and 10th, also emphasizes that the querent will be successful in the exam.

If the question is about getting a master's degree, again the 9th and 10th houses are considered. Lilly says "You must give the Ascendant to him of whom it is asked, and the 9th house to the *Science*; and if there be fortunes in the ninth house, or the Lord of the ninth fortunate, and behold the Lord of the Ascendant, judge there is Science in that man: But if in the ninth house there be *Infortunes*, or the Lord of the ninth unfortunate, and behold not the Lord of the Ascendant, it does signify the contrary, and that there is none, or little knowledge in him."[127]

As is obvious in Lilly's approach, the 9th house is also related to wisdom. Jupiter placed in this house may show the querent is on the path of becoming a wise man. The lord of the 9th in a conjunction, sextile, or trine with Jupiter also represents the same thing. The Moon or Sun in aspect with Jupiter is also considered. Religious and spiritual issues are represented by the 9th, and aspects of Jupiter promise wisdom.

If the question is related to success and promotion, the aspects of the Sun and Jupiter gain importance. Harmonious aspects between the lord of the Ascendant or the Moon with the Sun or Jupiter indicate prestige and success. If the lord of the Ascendant is in harmonious aspects with the Sun or Jupiter, or in conjunction with Jupiter, the querent becomes successful and gains prestige due to his higher education.

---

[127] Lilly, p. 430.

The difference between primary & higher education

In horary astrology, the 3rd house should be considered for questions related to primary education, whereas the 9th is related to questions about higher education. Graduate and post-graduate periods are related to the 9th, primary school and high school are related to the 3rd.

Short and long distance journeys

Astrology students may sometimes have problems with deciding on whether to use the 3rd or the 9th house for questions related to journeys. In principle, the 3rd pertains to short-distance journeys, and the 9th to long-distance ones. By analogy, the 3rd should be considered for inland journeys and the 9th house should be considered for journeys abroad.

In *The Martial Art of Horary Astrology*, Lee Lehman says that "The differences between 3rd and 9th are mental, not physical. All cities are 3rd House to some people and 9th House to others, just as all cities are home to residents and places to visit for everyone else."[128] Based on the principle of "familiarity," Lehman made the following kinds of distinctions:

- Third house people feel familiar in a place, can navigate it easily, know the local customs and services, and have some routine contact with its people and neighborhoods.
- Ninth house people feel unfamiliar in or discomfort in traveling to a place (even if they have been there before), need help navigating or understanding local customs and services, and feel like outsiders with few or no contacts.

---

[128] Lehman, p. 245.

QUESTIONS ON 10TH HOUSE MATTERS

Here I give practical advice on career and its changes, promotions, and professional talents.

Profession and career

Planets in the Ascendant, the lord of the Ascendant, and the Moon represent the querent; planets in the 10th and the lord of the 10th represent the profession, career, and success of the querent. An applying conjunction, sextile, or trine between the lord of the Ascendant and the lord of the 10th, or a collection or transfer of their light, indicates the querent will reach success in his profession, a promotion, or will get the job he wants. A collection or transfer of light shows that someone will contribute to this success.

If there is no applying aspect between the main significators (the lord of the Ascendant, the Moon, and the lord of the 10th) but there is a mutual reception or antiscion, the same interpretation is valid, while the opposite is true when there are negative aspects between the significators. Should there be a negative aspect with reception between the significators (by square or opposition), the querent reaches a positive result in spite of all difficulties and restrictions.

Benefics (Jupiter, Venus, the Sun, North Node, and the Lot of Fortune) placed in the 1st or 10th houses indicate that the querent will gain a promotion or attain success in his profession, or will get the job he asked for. Malefics (Saturn, Mars, the South Node) placed in the 1st or 10th show the querent will lose his job, be unsuccessful, will lose favor, or will not be able to get the job he wanted.

The lord of the 10th house in the 1st indicates the querent will easily gain success. However, the lord of the 1st placed in the 10th does not ensure success will come easily: it shows that the querent's mind is on his profession and success in his career. He has high expectations. However, when the lord of the Ascendant in this position makes a conjunction, sextile, or trine with the lord of the 10th, or is in a mutual reception, or has an antiscion relationship, the querent's chance for success is high. The lord of the Ascendant in that position having harmonious aspects with the Sun or Jupiter also brings great success and prestige.

Applying aspects of the lords of the Ascendant, Midheaven, or the Moon, with the Sun or Jupiter may represent both success and prestige. It may also indicate that the querent will get the job he wanted and then be successful in it. A conjunction or harmonious aspects between the lords of the Ascendant and/or Midheaven with Venus, the North Node, and the Lot of Fortune also bring success.

Positive aspects between the lords of the Ascendant and/or Midheaven and Mars or Saturn, when those malefic planets are in their dignity (or if they do not make any negative aspects with the other planets), mean the querent will gain the promotion, be successful, or get the job he wanted, but some inconveniences and challenges. However, negative aspects between the lords of the Ascendant or Midheaven and Mars or Saturn, or their applying conjunction with the South Node, mean the querent cannot obtain success and the job he wanted, and he will also experience difficulties and restrictions.

The lords of the Ascendant or Midheaven should be in their dignities and powerful. The powerful position of the lord of the Ascendant increases the power of the querent, and the strong position of the lord of the Midheaven increases success in career matters. Contacts between the lord of the Midheaven and the benefics are also positive. Positive aspects with the Sun also increase the chance of success.

The lord of the 10th placed in the 11th (which is related to hopes and wishes), may indicate the querent will get the job he wants or be successful. A conjunction, positive aspect, mutual reception, or antiscion between the lords of the 10th and 11th increases the chance of success.

The lord of the 10th placed in the 10th may again show the querent will get the job he wants, or will be successful, if it is not in negative aspects, especially with the malefics.

The lord of the 10th placed in one of the angular houses, or in harmonious aspects with the lords of the angular houses, increases the chance of success. The house ruled by the planet which is in harmonious aspect with the lord of the 10th also indicates the person from whom the querent can obtain support. For instance, if this planet rules the 11th, the querent will be supported by his friends and his social environment. But the house ruled by the planet in an inharmonious aspect with the lord of the 10th, indicates the person who will put some obstacles in the querent's path. For instance, if this planet rules the 6th, the querent will face problems and troubles due to his underlings, workers, the bad conditions of his place of work, or his bad health.

"When will I get the job I wanted?"

If the lord of the 10th is retrograde or slow in motion, the job that the querent gets will be with some delay or in the future. On the other hand, if the lord of the 10th is direct and quick in motion, the querent gets the job he wants within a short time.

The lord of the 10th in one of the angular houses indicates the querent will get the job he wants, or attain success quickly, if promised by the other significators. The lord of the 10th in one of the succedent houses indicates success within a middling period. But the lord of the 10th in one of the cadent houses shows a later time for reaching success (and the chance for success is low).

The quality of the signs in which the lord of the Ascendant, the lord of the 10th, or the lord of the sign of the Moon are placed, and their aspects should also be considered. Cardinal signs represent quick developments; mutable signs represent developments within the middle term, and fixed signs represent late developments. If mutable signs are dominant, the existing conditions may change later. This possibility is higher if the significator is retrograde.

"Shall I be dismissed?"

In the case of an applying square or opposition between the lord of the Ascendant and the lord of the 10th, or if the Moon is separating from a conjunction or negative aspect with one of these planets and applying to a conjunction or negative aspect with the other, the querent is under the risk of being dismissed.

The lord of the Ascendant or the 10th, or the Moon, applying to a conjunction or negative aspect with malefics (Saturn, Mars, the South Node) also indicates that the querent is under risk of being dismissed.

If the lord of the Midheaven is in one of the angular houses and especially in a fixed sign, we may conclude that the querent will not be dismissed. However, if this planet is in the last degrees of that fixed sign and about to enter a mutable sign, we may not make the same conclusion because the conditions seem to be changing.

If the querent is already gone from his job and asks if he will return or not, the lord of the Ascendant or Midheaven is retrograde and in an aspect with the Ascendant, the querent may return to his job. If the lord of the Ascendant is applying to a conjunction or positive aspect with the lord of the Midheaven, the querent may return to his job. If there is no aspect between the lords of the Ascendant and Midheaven but the Moon is transferring the light between them, or a third planet is collecting their light, the querent returns to his job with the help of others.

Changing jobs and transfers

For such questions, the lord of the 1st house and the Moon should be considered. William Lilly says, "If the Lord of the first or the Moon be joined to the Lord of the tenth or either of them, and he more weighty than either of them, and be in a good place of heaven, *viz.* either in the tenth, eleventh, or fifth free from all manner of impediments, though he behold not the tenth, yet not withstanding if the *querent* be in any Command or Office, he shall be transferred to some other place of trust or Command: But if he behold the tenth house, then he shall continue where he is."[129]

In such questions, if the fixed signs are on the axes of the chart and the main significators (like the lord of the Ascendant, the Moon, or the lord of the Midheaven) are in fixed signs, the possibility of changing jobs or transferring is low. Cardinal or mutable signs on the axes and the main significators likewise in cardinal or mutable signs reflect a higher chance for such a change or transfer.

The lord of the Ascendant in the last degrees of its sign indicate that the querent's conditions will change in the near future; the lord of the Midheaven in the same situation indicates that the working conditions or the type of job will change. The Moon in this situation shows that the course of events is about to change. If one of the significators is about to shift from a fixed sign into a mutable sign, the existing conditions will change. If one shifts from a cardinal sign to a fixed one, a decision has just been made and the conditions will be fixed. If one of the significators is shifting from a mutable sign to a cardinal one, the changing and indefinite conditions are now about to be decided.

"Which job should I choose?"

For such a question, if it is about the profession in general, the natal chart should be the key. However, for specific questions about a certain job, a horary chart can be used. Answering such questions may also be valuable for querents who do not know their birth dates or the exact time of birth.

---

[129] Lilly, p. 448.

Here, the nature and significations of the sign on the 10th house, and the sign and house where the lord of the 10th is, should be considered (such as Scorpio indicating a psychologist, or the lord of the 10th in the 9th indicating an academic). If there is any planet in the 10th house, the nature of the planet may help to determine the proper profession for the querent (such as the Moon in the 10th indicating a genealogist because of the Moon's indications for family).

Another method is to determine the significators of two alternatives and to consider the most powerful one of them. For instance, the querent may need to decide between working in trade and business, or the arts. So, Mercury (as the representative of commerce) and Venus (as the representative of arts) should be compared as to their strengths.

Government and officials

In a horary chart, the 10th house is considered for questions about the government and officials in authority. Planets in the 10th and the lord of the 10th represent the government, officials, and authority figures. If the querent is an authority figure and asking a question about his own achievement, then this person is represented by the 1st, not the 10th.

If the question is whether a politician will be successful or not, or whether or not someone will climb to a higher status, the quaesited is represented by the 10th or the Sun. If the quaesited official, politician, or manager is a woman, the Moon may also be considered. However, we should keep in mind that managers and well-known people are always represented by the Sun.

If the question is about which of two political parties will win the election, the ruling party or its leader is represented by the 10th house, and the opposition party or the leader of the opposition by the 4th.

For questions about benefits or support expected from the government, the 11th house should also be considered in addition to the 10th, because the 11th represents the funds of the government. A positive aspect or conjunction between the lord of the Ascendant (the significator of the querent) or the Moon (the course of the events) and the lord of the 11th shows the benefit which is desired from the government, or that a person in authority will arrive.

Inharmonious aspects between the lord of the Ascendant or the Moon and the lord of the 11th, show that the support will not be received. Notwithstanding a negative aspect between the significators, if there is a mutual reception the support will arrive after having to deal with some difficulties and restrictions.

If the significators are not in strong positions, the support may be lower than expected.

"Should I be self-employed or work for others?"

For such questions we should consider whether the main significators are in the 10th house or in aspect with the lord of the 10th, or if they are in the 6th or in aspect with the lord of the 6th. The emphasis on the 10th house or contacts with the lord of the 10th, requires a judgment that the querent should work at his own business, while the emphasis on the 6th house, or contacts with the lord of the 6th, indicates the querent should work for others.

The natal chart is the proper foundation for such questions. However, the querent who should be self-employed may not be ready for this at the time, or he may be advised to work for others for a while. The greatest benefit of horary charts is to give us answers on specific questions.

QUESTIONS ON 11TH HOUSE MATTERS

This section addresses questions related to hopes and expectations, friends, social groups, and organizations.

Hopes and expectations

Planets in the Ascendant, the lord of the Ascendant, and the Moon represent the querent; planets in the 11th and the lord of the 11th represent the thing that the querent hopes for or expects. An applying conjunction, sextile, or trine between these significators shows the querent will attain his wishes. If there is no aspect or conjunction between the lord of the Ascendant (or planets in the Ascendant) and the lord of the 11th house (or planets in it), but the Moon is transferring the light between them or a slow-moving third planet is collecting the light of these significators, the querent attains his wishes through the help of other people.

The lord of the 11th in a strong position, in one of the angular houses and in its own dignity, indicates that what the querent hoped or wished for is important and realizable. If however it does not have any aspects with the querent's main significators (planets in the Ascendant, the lord of the Ascendant, and the Moon), the querent may not attain the thing he asked for. The lord of the 11th placed in the 11th is an advantageous position. However, in order to judge that the querent will reach his wishes, there should be an aspect or reception or antiscion between the significators.

The lord of the 11th placed in the 1st is one of the most advantageous placements. If the other factors do not represent despair, the querent attains his wishes. The lord of the 1st placed in the 11th does not automatically assure that the querent will attain his wishes, so the other factors should be supportive.

If the querent hopes to get financial or spiritual support from an important person, again the lord of the 11th is considered together with the above-mentioned conditions. If there are negative aspects between the significators, then it is hard for the querent to attain his wishes. In spite of any negative aspects, if there is mutual reception between the significators the querent attains his wishes after some difficulties and delays.

Benefics (Jupiter, Venus, the Sun, North Node, and the Lot of Fortune) placed in the 11th house show that what is hoped for will be realized, if the other factors do not indicate the contrary. Benefics should be considered in terms of dignity and their aspects. For instance, if Jupiter is in detriment or in fall in the 11th house, if he is in negative aspects with the other significators, retrograde or burned, the querent cannot realize his wishes as much as he had hoped.

Malefics (Saturn, Mars, the South Node) placed in the 11th house indicate that what is hoped for will not be realized, if the other factors do not represent the contrary. Again, the malefics should be considered in terms of dignity and their aspects. For instance, if Saturn is in dignity, in the 11th, and in positive aspects with the other planets, the querent may attain his wishes after experiencing some difficulties and delays.

According to Lilly, in terms of reception in mutable signs, the querent's wish is attained partially. He says: "If the same Receiver be in a movable Sign, he shall only have the name, or a probability of having thereof, or else very little of it."[130] He adds, "Note, if anyone ask for a thing secretly, saying, *Look, I pray you for me, If I shall obtain the thing I hope for, or not*: consider if you find the Lord of the ascendant and the Moon applying to *Fortunes*, and in angles or Succedents, then he shall obtain it, otherwise not. But if the *querent* shall manifest the thing and name it, then you must behold the thing in its own proper place pertaining to the same House, and so judge of the hopes or not hopes thereof."[131]

---

[130] Lilly, p. 458.
[131] Lilly, p. 459.

Friends

If the question is about getting along and forming a business or organization with friends, again the 11th house is considered. If there are harmonious aspects between planets in the Ascendant, the lord of the Ascendant, or the Moon, and planets in the 11th or the lord of the 11th, the querent will obtain positive outcomes from the business and ventures with his friends, he will make peace if there is any resentment, or will get the thing he hoped for from his friend.

If there is no aspect between the main significators, but the Moon is transferring the light between them, or if another planet is collecting the light of the lord of the Ascendant and the lord of the 11th, then a third person may contribute to the positive relationship between the querent and his friend. The querent receives the help or the thing that he wanted to get from his friend, through the help of another person.

If there is resentment between friends and the question is whether or not they will make peace, then in addition to the aspects of the Ascendant and the lord of the 11th we should also consider if the Moon is applying to a conjunction or positive aspect with Venus. An applying conjunction or positive aspect between the Moon and Venus show the parties will make peace. If the applying aspect is a negative one, the parties do not make peace. The Moon and Venus in negative aspect but in reception (like Venus in Cancer and the Moon in Libra) means that the parties make peace after some struggles and difficulties.

Malefics in the 11th indicate the friendship will be damaged. If one of the malefics is placed on the Ascendant, the problem stems from the querent; if one of the malefics is placed in the 11th, the problem stems from the querent's friend (the quaesited).

The Moon applying to an aspect or conjunction with a malefic indicates the querent will have problems connected to his friends. The Moon applying to an aspect or conjunction with a benefic indicates the querent will benefit from his friend, will get the desired support from his friend, or the friendship will survive.

Charities, parties, and organizations

Again the 11th house, the planets in it, and the lord of the 11th are considered. Even if the question is about the success of business organizations, the same rules apply.

If the querent asks whether or not joining an organization or party is beneficial for him, benefics in the 11th indicate this venture will be beneficial. The opposite is true when the malefics are in this house. If the malefics are in their dignities, provided that they are not in negative aspects with other planets, we may again conclude that this venture will be beneficial for the querent.

The lord of the Ascendant applying to a positive aspect with the lord of the 11th shows that the querent will benefit from the social environment he is about to enter. The lord of the Ascendant or the Moon applying to a positive aspect or conjunction with the Sun or Jupiter, indicates the querent will meet with powerful and respectful people and will benefit from them. He may even become stronger and respected due to his relationship with them. If there is not an applying conjunction or positive aspect between the lord of the Ascendant and the lord of the 11th, but the Moon or another third planet is transferring or collecting the light, the positive developments occur through the help of other people. On the other hand, if the lord of the Ascendant is about to make a conjunction, square, or opposition with one of the malefics, or if the Moon is transferring the light between these two planets to by conjunction or a negative aspect, the querent experiences some negative developments through the intervention of some events or some people.

If the question is about a party, charity, or club, then planets in the 11th and the upcoming aspects of the lord of the 11th represent the direction of the events for the organization or institution. The

Sun, Venus, Jupiter, North Node, or Lot of Fortune placed in the 11th represents a great success. On the other hand, Saturn, Mars, or the South Node in the 11th represents failure.

QUESTIONS ON 12TH HOUSE MATTERS

This pertains to hidden hostilities, and people in prisons and hospitals.

Questions about hidden enemies

The 12th house answers these questions, as it is related to people who are unknown, cause problems, and create negativity behind the scenes. If the querent knows the person who is creating the problem, the 7th house (the house of open enemies) should be considered.[132]

The querent is represented by the lord of the Ascendant, the planets in the 1st house, and the Moon. The quaesited, the hidden enemy, is represented by the lord of the 12th and planets in that house. If the approaching aspect between these significators is negative, the hidden enemy or the person who is creating problems behind the scenes will be harmful for the querent. A malefic in the 12th house also increases this possibility. However, if they do not have any aspects with the lord of the Ascendant or the Moon, they will not be harmful for the querent. The significator of the querent entering into burning is the worst condition: the querent may be harmed, especially if the Sun is the lord of the 12th and the planet which is entering into burning is the lord of the Ascendant. If the lord of the 12th makes a negative aspect to the lord of the Ascendant from the 6th, 8th, or 12th houses, it is obvious that someone is willing to do mischief to the querent.[133]

---

[132] Lilly, p. 460.
[133] Lilly, p. 460.

"Who is trying to disturb things?"

To determine who the hidden enemy is, or the one making trouble behind the scenes, the planet placed in the 12th house is considered. If Mercury is in the 12th, the hidden enemy may be a young and talkative person; if Venus, a young lady or a sister; if the Sun, a male figure, boss, or person in authority.

The house ruled by the planet in the 12th may also be considered for this question. If the planet in the 12th house is the lord of the 3rd, the hidden enemy may be a sibling or neighbor. If it is the lord of the 6th, the servants; if the lord of the 11th, someone from his social circle may be the hidden enemy.

Another way to answer this question is through the house which the lord of the 12th is in. If the lord of the 12th is in the 6th, the hidden enemy is someone from the work environment or colleagues; if in the 3rd, someone from his inner circle and somewhere near; in the 9th, the hidden enemy may be in a far distant place, or from academia, or the reason for the hostility may be related to beliefs. As the lord of the 12th house indicates the hidden enemy, if this significator is in a weak position the hidden enemy is also weak and cannot harm to the querent. The same is true if the significator of the querent is strongly placed. If the lord of the Ascendant is in a stronger position than the lord of the 12th, or is in its dignity, or placed in a stronger house of the chart, the querent will not be damaged by the quaesited or this secret enemy. If the Sun is the significator of the querent, or if the lord of the 12th house is burned, the querent will dominate his secret enemy.

"Shall I be imprisoned or hospitalized?"

The 12th house should be considered because confinement is one of the matters ruled by it. Hospitals, prisons, sanatoriums, and nursing homes are within the scope of the 12th house.

In the chart of such a question, if the lord of the Ascendant is in the 12th, if it has negative aspects, or is burned, the querent may be imprisoned or hospitalized. The Moon in the 12th does not mean the querent will be imprisoned or hospitalized, but it represents a great deal of anxiety.

When the querent is already imprisoned or hospitalized, if the lord of the Ascendant is in the 12th house, in a fixed sign, retrograde, slow in motion, the querent may have to stay in prison or hospital for a long time. On the other hand, if the lord of the Ascendant is in a cardinal sign, in quick in motion, direct, and if the Moon is also quick in motion, the querent may get out of the prison or hospital quickly. Any planet (especially the lord of the Ascendant or the lord of the 12th) in the last degrees of the 12th house, and being close to the degree of the Ascendant, also indicates the same thing, if it is not retrograde.

Lilly adds, "You should also note, that the Quarters of Heaven in the Figure, are of great strength and force; for the *Significators* in Quarters feminine, do signify a swift going out, the other more slow: so also common signs show a time between both; for if the *Significator* be in one of them, it signifies he shall be imprisoned again."[134] Mutable signs represent repeating or changing conditions.

It is beneficial for the querent if the lord of the Ascendant is not in the 4th, 6th, 8th, or 12th houses, because they represent difficulties related to imprisonment. The 4th house is related to being imprisoned.

The Moon or the lord of the Moon in contact with one of the benefics may show the querent will be released from the prison soon.[135]

The lord of the 12th in the 1st may bring imprisonment or hospitalization. It at least indicates that the querent will be faced with negative conditions.

---

[134] Lilly, p. 461.
[135] Lilly, p. 462.

7: EXAMPLE CHARTS

Here are some example questions and answers from my case notes. In the years that have elapsed since them, I have learned how the events in them developed afterwards, sometimes in surprising ways. After seeing this correspondence between the charts and events, my trust in this ancient branch of astrology increased. I still get new questions from my clients and answer them using the techniques we have inherited from the ancient scholars.

"Will the threat turn out badly?"

The querent was a businessman, and was being threatened by someone with whom he had had business dealings. The person threatening the querent was living in another city and engaged in trade. As this other man's work had not been going well for a while, he was deeply depressed.

Although he was married, he was having a love affair with another woman and that was also not going well. Being thus in the middle of chaotic and negative events in many fields of life, this other man went mad, killed two people, and ran away in a panic. He was sought by the police. He thought he had killed the two people because of his business relationship with the querent, and blamed him. He called the querent a few times and threatened him by saying, "I killed two people and I can kill another. You are the next. I will kill you, too." The querent was very anxious when he told me about this case on the phone. He asked me, "Will he really do what he said? Will this threat turn out badly? Will he kill me?" I erected a horary chart, examined it carefully and told him there were some indicators which shows that he should be careful, we could not know exactly what will happen but he should take the necessary precautions.

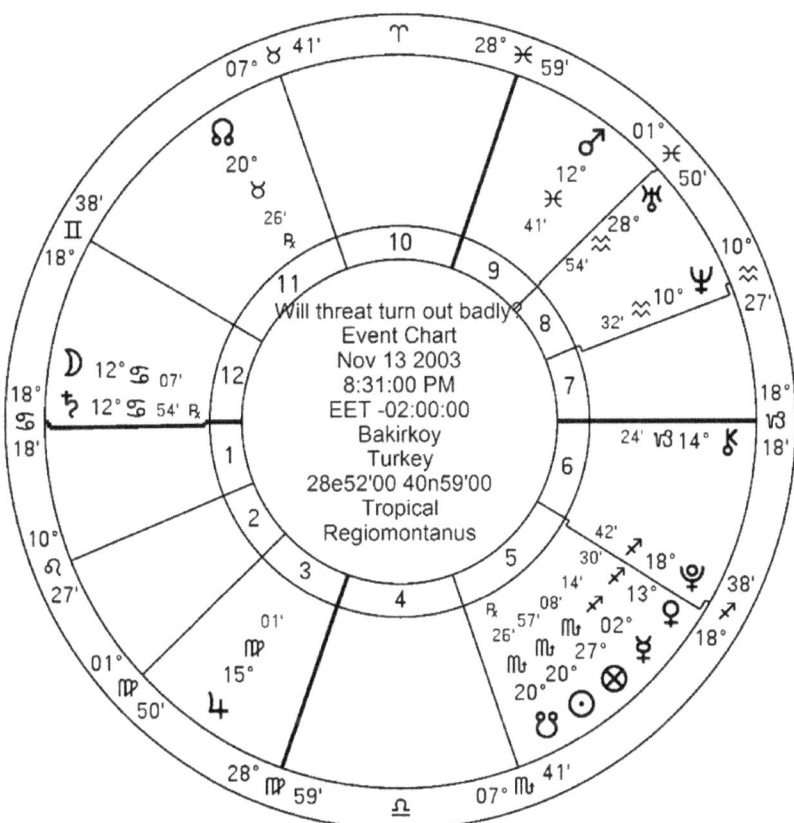

Figure 15: Will the threat turn out badly?

In this chart (Figure 15), Cancer was rising. The Moon, signifying the querent (as the lord of the Ascendant), was in the 12th house of hidden enemies, and was about to conjoin with Saturn, the lord of the 7th house (open enemies). The distance between these two was less than 1°, meaning that the conjunction would become exact within a short period of time. This showed that the hidden enemies would be quickly apparent. Based on this indication, I told the querent that he would meet the man who threatened him within a very short time; perhaps they would have a secret meeting. I also told him that this man would be very close to him; perhaps he would be hiding somewhere and would go into action soon.

The Moon as the significator of the querent was in a strong position when compared to Saturn: in short, the querent was stronger than his enemy. However, the Moon was currently in the 12th house of the chart, which meant that it would take some time for the querent to have a sigh of relief. The Moon was 6° behind the Ascendant and in a cardinal sign, but in a house where she is not that comfortable. Under these conditions we could conclude that the querent would feel comfortable six months or weeks later. The querent was so anxious about this threat that he could not even go to his office for a few weeks and preferred staying at home. He also went to the police to report the threat he had received, and even hired a personal security guard for himself.

The toughest situation in this chart was that the Moon's next conjunction was with Saturn. On the other hand, the Moon would make beneficial aspects immediately afterwards: this indicated that the situation would calm down within the coming days. Nevertheless, the Moon-Saturn conjunction showed that he would be in danger if he was not careful enough.

I called the querent and told him that he should go to the police and be very careful. After a while, the querent told me he had learned that the man who threatened him was hiding in a flat only two streets away: he was preparing to assassinate the querent. However, he left that place when he learned that his address had been detected by the police.

The threats continued for a while. As seen in the chart, the querent did not feel secure for nearly six months. On some days he could not even go to his office because of the threatening calls he received. He was concerned the man would harm his colleagues and employees. The Saturn in the question chart transiting in the querent's natal 6th house also indicated such setbacks and his concerns about his employees. Neptune, transiting from the degree of the natal Ascendant, also represented the anxiety which heavily influenced the querent. In his 2003 solar revolution chart, Uranus was close to the Sun in the 7th house, the house of open enemies. This also suggested that querent was open to unexpected developments and hostility related to male figures. In his chart for 2004 Mars stood at the cusp of the 7th house, indicating that the threats would continue for a while. The threats continued a while longer but then stopped. The man was finally arrested by the police.

The risk was obvious; fortunately, the worst fears did not come true. As William Lilly said, "If the significator of the querent is applying to malefics, the querent is right to feel afraid; while the significator of the querent is applying to a benefic and is not in reception with a malefic, there is no need to feel afraid. If the Moon is in the 8th, 6th, or 12th houses and applying to a planet in a cadent house, again there is no need to worry or the things will be back on track even after a while. When the Moon makes trine with the Sun, the problems are solved immediately." The Moon-Saturn conjunction in the 12th, Moon being in Cancer and then making good aspects with Mars and Jupiter, and finally making a trine with the Sun, explains why this threat did not lead to a negative outcome.

"Will I be appointed to another school?"

A high school teacher asked me if she would be appointed to another school or not. She also added that the situation was going to be clarified in August or September.

When I erected the chart (see Figure 16), the first thing that attracted my attention was the axes of the chart, all in fixed signs. This position generally indicates that the condition of the querent will not change. However, I discovered other points as I went on examining the chart. For example, the Sun being the lord of the Ascendant and representing the querent was at the end of Taurus (a fixed sign) and was about to enter Gemini, a mutable sign. The Sun was also placed in the 10th house. This placement showed that the fixed position of the querent (the Sun as the lord of the Ascendant) was about to change and this change was related to the querent's career. The querent had been working at a school for a long time. The position of the Sun showed that she was about to complete her job there and be appointed to another place. Venus (the lord of the Midheaven, representing career and reputation) was in a mutable sign, Gemini. Mutable signs represent changing conditions.

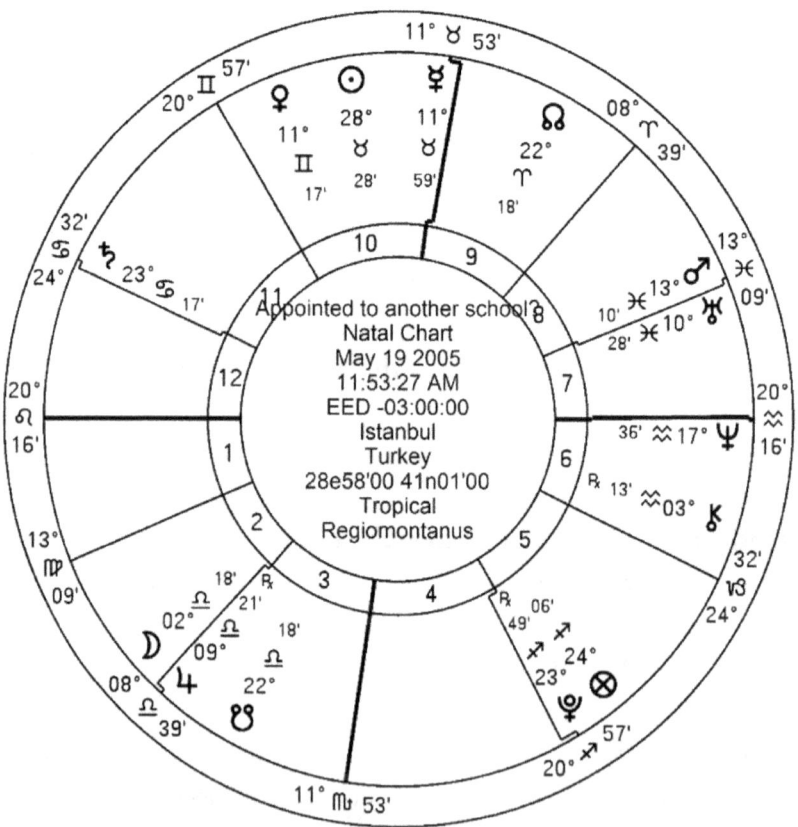

Figure 16: Will I be appointed to another school?

The Moon, which represents the course of events, was in Libra, a cardinal sign, and was about to conjoin with Jupiter, who was retrograding in the same sign. Cardinal signs are related to taking action and initiative. Based on those significators, I predicted that she would be appointed to another school.

Another indicator of this appointment was that the Moon was going to make a trine with Venus after her conjunction with Jupiter. This appointment would also be very beneficial for the querent and bring ease to her life. The querent had a daughter and she wanted her to attend the same school. As Jupiter (in conjunction with the Moon) was the lord of the 5th, the possibility for the querent and her daughter to go to the same school was really high. However, as Jupiter was retrograde there would be some delays.

Next, I examined when the planets changed signs and the upcoming aspects of the Moon, in order to determine the timing of this appointment. The Sun was about to change signs after 1.5°. There was another important significator: the Moon was about to make a conjunction with the retrograding Jupiter in Libra within 7°. This conjunction would be in Libra, a cardinal sign, and in the 3rd house (a cadent house), which indicated a period of seven months. The trine between the Moon and Venus, the lord of the Midheaven, would be exact after 9°: since Venus is in an angular house and a mutable sign, and the Moon is close to the cusp of the 3rd and in a cardinal sign, her appointment would take place after approximately nine months.

As the next aspect of the Moon was her conjunction with Jupiter in a cardinal sign, I predicted that she would be appointed to another school seven months later. This sounded strange to her because the schools were opening in September and there were only four months until then. Interestingly, her appointment took more time than expected and she started working in her new school in December. A planet in retrograde motion shows that the event will take place before or after (usually after) it is expected, or it will take place in a different way than expected. The querent was not hopeful when she asked the question. On the other hand, as another teacher from the school she hoped to be appointed to wanted to work in another place, due to this opening she began working in this school very unexpectedly.

"Should I continue working at my current company?"

The querent was working at a telecommunications company in a managerial position, but was thinking of changing the company he worked for because the existing conditions did not satisfy him well enough. He had an opportunity to work at a public company and was not sure if he should take this opportunity or continue working in his current company. He asked me: "Should I stay in this current company?"

When the question is about changing jobs, we should examine the axes of the chart. In this chart (see Figure 17) the axes of the chart are in cardinal signs, reflecting that the querent should take the initiative and wants to take some steps to make changes. On the other hand, the two lords of the Ascendant (the sign lord Mars and exalted lord the Sun) were in fixed signs. Saturn, the lord of the Midheaven, and Mars (the victor of the Midheaven) were also in fixed signs. This showed that changing jobs would be difficult or that the querent should not prefer to change his current situation. Mars as the lord of the Ascendant, representing the querent, was in the 2nd house, indicating that the querent would prioritize his financial position and would not want to change jobs. Saturn, being the significator of his career as the lord of the Midheaven, was in a fixed sign and also in retrograde motion. This position showed that even if the querent wanted to change jobs, the conditions would not permit such a change, or delays would occur.

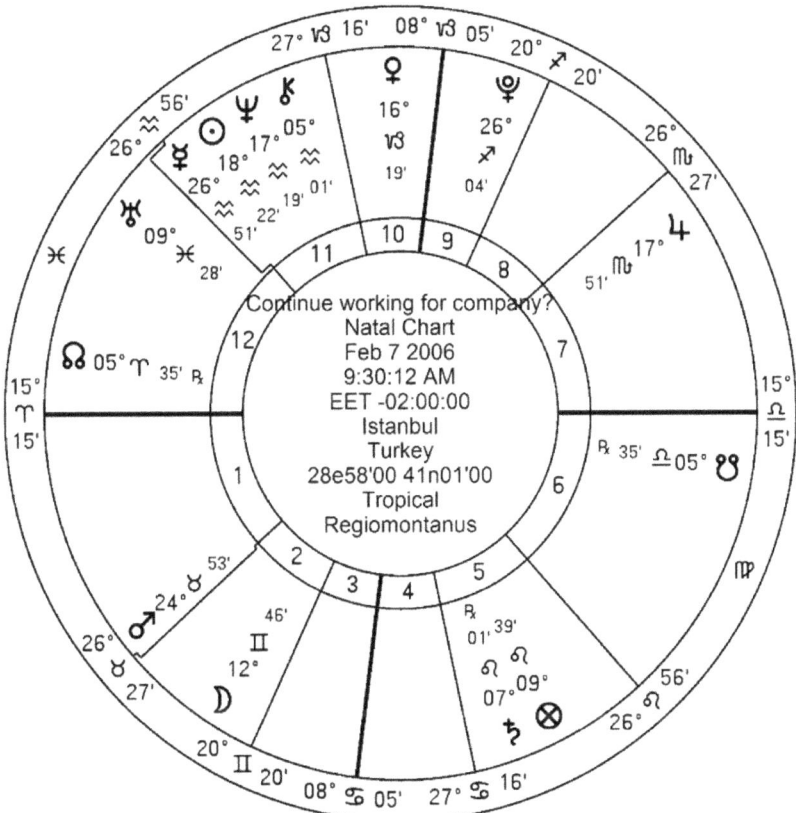

Figure 17: Should I continue working at my current company?

When a question is related to career and status, the Sun is an important significator. The Sun also represents authority figures (managers, directors, etc.). The Sun's first applying aspect will be a square to Mars (the victor of the Midheaven and the lord of the 8th house), which will be exact in 6.5°. As these two planets were both in fixed signs and succedent houses, I predicted that the querent would have some difficulties and have to leave after 6.5 months or 6.5 years, if he stayed in his existing job. Consequently, the querent decided to stay in his existing company. However, the telecommunication company he was working decided to downsize and announced that the employees who were qualified for retirement would be laid off. As the querent was qualified for retirement, he had to retire as of January 28, 2013—approximately seven years after he asked me this question, as I had stated!

"Will the catering job with my friends keep going?"

The querent was living in the USA and running a catering business with friends from Turkey (see Figure 18). The significator of the querent in the 11th house in Cancer showed that this question was radical. Taurus (whose nature signifies the catering business), was also in the 10th house. Venus, which is related to the dining industry, was also in the 10th. (The Moon is the other significator related to the dining industry.)

As the question was also about the querent's friends, the planets located in the 11th house were also indications that this chart was radical. The querent told me that he was involved in business with two friends. The Sun (the lord of the Ascendant), Saturn, and Mercury were placed in the 11th house. So I asked the querent, "Does one of those friends, who is not talented enough and a clumsy one, slow down the business?" The querent answered surprisingly "Yes!" I was describing to him the qualities of Saturn in Cancer. Then I went on, asking: "And the other one is talented and smart and has very strong communication skills, but you do not see enough performance from him, is it right?" The querent was surprised again and said "Yes!" What I had described to the querent was Mercury peregrine in Cancer. While interpreting natal charts and horary charts, by asking questions of the native or the querent, you may help them realize the astrological symbolism and witness how magnificent astrology is!

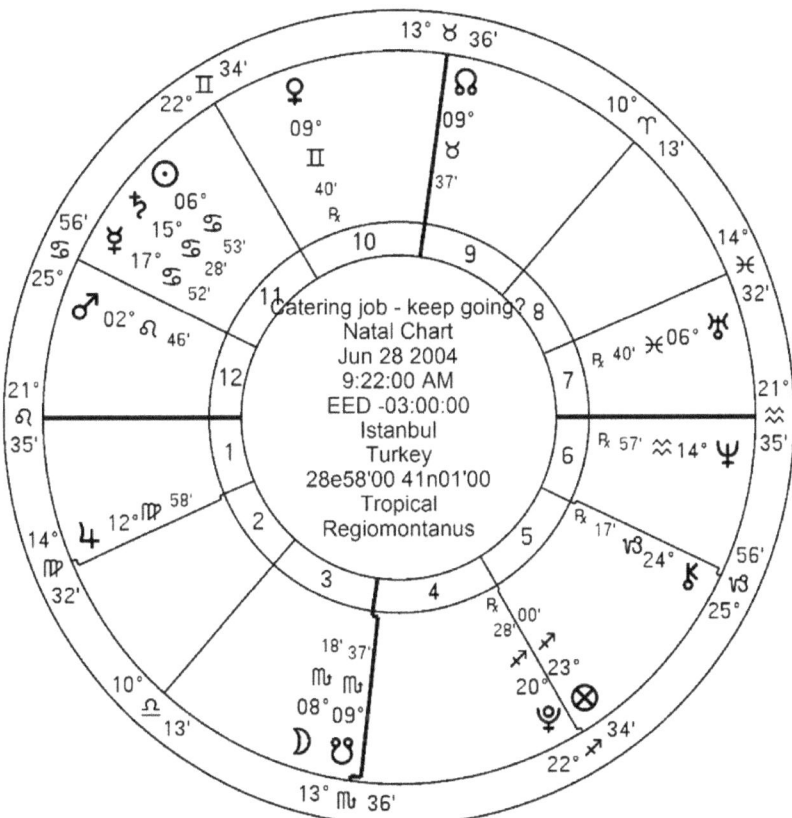

Figure 18: Will the catering job with my friends keep going?

Those questions gave me confidence regarding the significators and I was able to understand the capabilities of the querent's business partners. The significator of the querent, the Sun, was also peregrine in Cancer. Moreover the Moon, the lord of Cancer (where they were), was in her fall in Scorpio and damaged due to her conjunction with the South Node. This showed me that the querent's capacity for carrying on this business were limited.

The axes of the chart were in fixed signs, showing the business would continue. The Moon in a fixed sign also showed the same thing. However, the significators of the querent and his friends were in cardinal signs. Venus, the lord of the Midheaven and significator of career, was in a mutable sign and in retrograde motion. Those significators indicated that carrying on with this business would be difficult; the conditions, or the course of the business, would change.

So, there were both positive and negative significations in the chart. As I mentioned before, the Sun was peregrine, showing that the querent was inadequate and had difficulties in managing and directing the course of the business. He was applying to a sextile with Jupiter, a positive signification. The Moon was also transferring the light of these two planets. The Moon, ruling Saturn and Mercury, would carry the light between the Sun (the querent) and his friends (Mercury, as lord of the 11th). As the Moon was applying to positive aspects, I thought that the business might continue and bring profit. However, the Moon-South Node conjunction, being the first aspect which will take place immediately, represented serious problems and the risk of loss.

Another eye-catching point in the chart was Mercury, the significator of the querent's friends, separated from Saturn by 2° and moving towards the 12th house: it seemed one of the friends would leave the business. This really happened. The friend whom I identified with Mercury left the business a while after this question. Then his other friend, identified with Saturn, left the partnership. As the Moon, being the lord of the friends' significators (in Cancer), was close to a conjunction with the South Node, it showed that the friends would leave the business and bring some negative developments. The Moon was also the lord of the Sun (the significator of the querent), and showed that the querent would not stay in the business, either. The Moon – South Node conjunction would be exact after 1.5°, and it was in a fixed sign and cadent house. (Being close to the cusp of the 4th house, they might also be considered to be in an angular house.) Due to this position, I thought that he would end this business 1.5 years later and I shared my thoughts with the querent. I also informed him that if he insisted on running the business he would suffer damage and have troubles. This really happened! The querent tried to stay in the business after the departure of his friends, and while he earned some money he was not that successful and left the business by the beginning of 2006, approximately one and-a-half years after his question.

"Will we make a profit from the business with my siblings?"

The querent had a jewelry store at the Grand Bazaar in Istanbul (see Figure 19). He told me that he was not making the money he desired from the jewelry business he had with his siblings. He asked "Will we make a profit from the business I have with my siblings?"

Cancer, representing the family business, was rising at the time of the question, and four planets were placed in the 12th house. The Moon (the significator of the querent) was also placed in the 12th and was peregrine in Gemini. All of those significators pointed to loss, instead of profit! The weak placement of the Moon also showed that the querent's ability to influence the course of the business was low. The answer of the question seemed obvious; however, I went on examining the chart because there were some positive indicators.

Then I examined the aspects she was going to make, because those would show the future events that the querent would experience, and the course of those events. The first aspect of the Moon was a conjunction with Venus. Although Venus is a benefic planet, she was peregrine in Gemini and also weak in the 12th house; so that was not powerful enough. The business would go well for a while, but it would not be that profitable and would not last long because the conjunction would be in a cadent house, in a mutable sign, and also in the sign where both the Moon and Venus were peregrine. The real problem would occur when the Moon and Mars would conjoin and oppose Pluto. The business seemed to continue for one and-a-half months (or years), as the Moon was close to Venus by 1.5°, and then everything would get worse. The Moon would conjoin with Mars after 6° and would oppose Pluto after 7°.

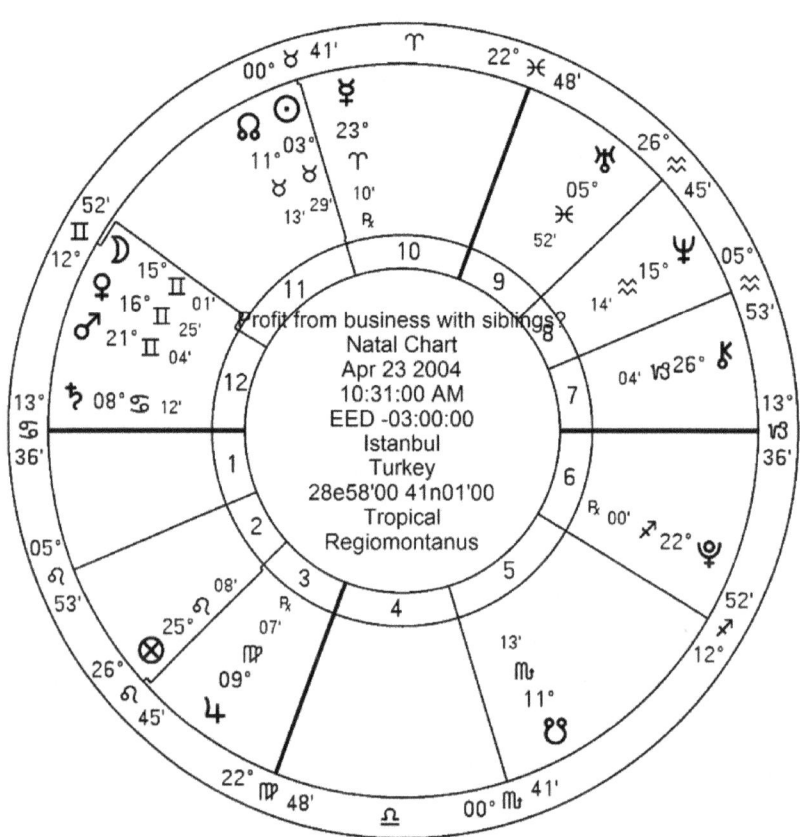

Figure 19: Will we make a profit from the business with my siblings?

I predicted that the events would occur 6 and 7 months later, and then there would be problems related to events behind the scenes (Mars in the 12th) and connected with the co-workers (Pluto in the 6th). Mercury (a significator of communication) was retrograding in the 10th at the time of the question, showing that some changes, misunderstandings, and miscalculations would bring problems.

As I mentioned before, there were some positive indications in the chart. Let's have a look of them and explain why they worked against the interests of the querent. The Lot of Fortune was placed close to the cusp of the 3rd house, and the Sun, the lord of the 3rd house, was in Taurus and the 11th house. Although the Sun was peregrine in Taurus, he was about to make a conjunction with the North Node. These factors showed that the querent would benefit (the Sun, being the lord of the 3rd house and the Lot of Fortune, placed in the 11th house, represents profit from the career), and he would do so from the jewelry production business (the Lot of Fortune in Leo signifies precious metals, Taurus indicates manufacture). Jupiter placed in the 3rd house indicates that the siblings were another positive indicator. Jupiter was also the lord of the 10th house, ruling the career. On the other hand, Jupiter retrograding and being in Virgo where he is damaged, showed that this business with the siblings would not bring the profit expected. Moreover, the Sun (in the 10th and lord of the 2nd, income) is mutually applying by trine with Jupiter in the 3rd house, so he is handing over his matter to this difficult Jupiter.

Although there were many positive factors, the planets placed in the 12th affected the positive outcome negatively. Jupiter (the lord of the Midheaven) and Mercury both retrograde also showed the business did not promise a good profit. So I told the querent that he would only gain a little money from the business and advised him to be careful about behind-the-scenes intrigues. After continuing this jewelry production business with his siblings for a while, the querent left and continued selling jewelry in his own store in the Grand Bazaar.

"Will my friend get the job she wants?"

One of my wife's friends was applying for other career opportunities, as she was unhappy with her job and had some problems with her current boss. She applied for a managerial position in a company operating in the publishing industry, and was called for an interview. She wanted this job. On the day of her interview, my wife saw her desire and excitement for the job and wondered if her friend would get it or not. She asked me the question: "Will my friend get this job she wants so much?"

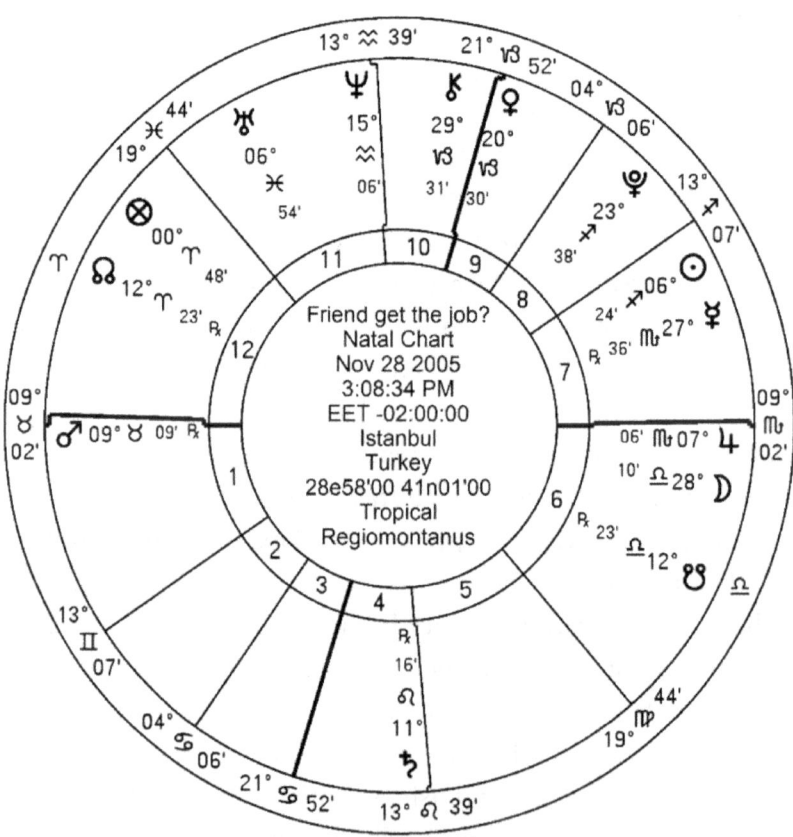

Figure 20: Will my friend get the job she wants?

Mars rising in Taurus at the moment of the question showed that the answer was "no" (see Figure 20). A malefic planet close to the Ascendant indicates the answer of the question is negative. Mars, the lord of the 9th house (publishing) from the 11th house (the friend), and the lord of its 2nd house, (the friend's income)[136] was also in retrograde motion. Mercury's position showed that the interview would not go well and would be unsatisfactory.

Saturn was the significator of my wife's friend, as the lord of the 11th. Saturn was retrograde and in detriment at the cusp of the 5th, which was the 7th house (interviews) from the 11th house. This position showed that my wife's friend was not adequate for this job and would not get what she desired.

Saturn's first aspect was a square with Jupiter. This square was important because Jupiter was the lord of Sagittarius, the 10th house from the 11th house (the friend's profession). All those significators showed that my wife's friend would not get this job. As Jupiter was the lord of Pisces, the 2nd house from the 11th house, she would not be satisfied with the salary she would be offered. On the other hand, Jupiter was not in dignity in Scorpio, and his first aspect was with the malefic, retrograde Mars in detriment. (It is true that Mars is receiving Jupiter, but I did not take this to mean the result would actually be converted into good.)

Moreover, the Moon was void in course at the time of the question. Based on those indications I told my wife: "I don't think that she will get this job." This turned out to be true.

---

[136] **BD**: This is because Aries (ruled by Mars) is intercepted in the friend's 2nd house.

"Where is my friend's son?"

The querent's son had been missing since Sunday night, January 14th, 2007. His family and the querent were very anxious. I saw the question in the forum page of our website (which was active then), erected a chart for the time when I read the question, and began examining it (see Figure 21).

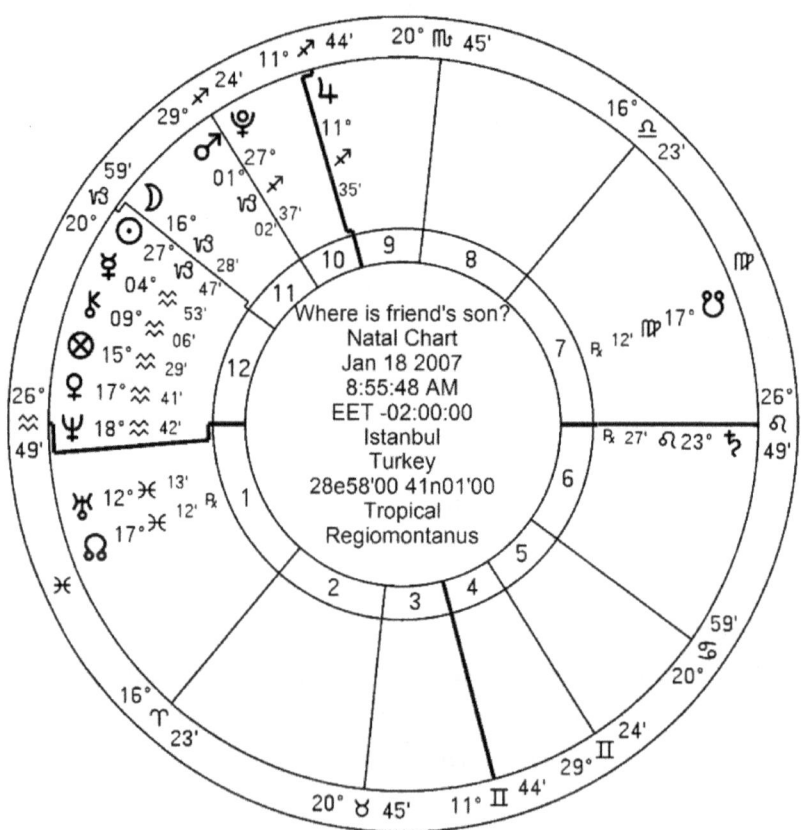

Figure 21: Where is my friend's son?

Aquarius was rising in the chart. As the question was about a friend's son of the querent, I looked at Taurus, which was on the cusp of the 5th house (child) from the 11th house (friend): this was the 3rd house of the chart itself. Venus, the lord of this house and representing the child, was in Aquarius and the 12th, about to conjoin with Neptune. This conjunction showed that it would be hard to find the child and there was something dubious about the situation. After that conjunction, Venus was going to make an opposition with Saturn. This was a malefic aspect showing that finding the child in a safe and sound condition would be hopeless. The Moon was waning, adding despair. The 12th house was highly crowded: this also pointed out that there was no hope for finding the child.

Then, where could the child be? Venus (the significator of the child) was in Aquarius, showing the west as the direction. The 12th house where Venus was placed, represents hidden places, hospitals, dens, the place of hidden enemies, where people hide, and places where cattle live. Could the child be in such places?

The Moon (the general significator of the event) was waning and about to go under the rays. This indicates that there is an obscurity and the energy is low. It was certain that something was about to end. Venus, which would apply to the opposition of Neptune and Saturn and the planets gathered in the 12th house, signified that the child would not be found or his dead body would be found.

In the end, nothing was ever heard about the child and he was never found.

"Will we set up this astrology website? What is the problem?"

I asked this question myself (see Figure 22). I was about to set up an astrology website with some of my friends, where we would publish articles on astrology. We had many meetings about it but could not reach a conclusion. So I asked my question: "Will we set up this astrology website?"

Sagittarius (the natural ninth sign of the zodiac, indicating media and publishing) rising showed the question was a radical one. Pluto placed close to the Ascendant signified that this website would bring some challenges and manipulative situations.

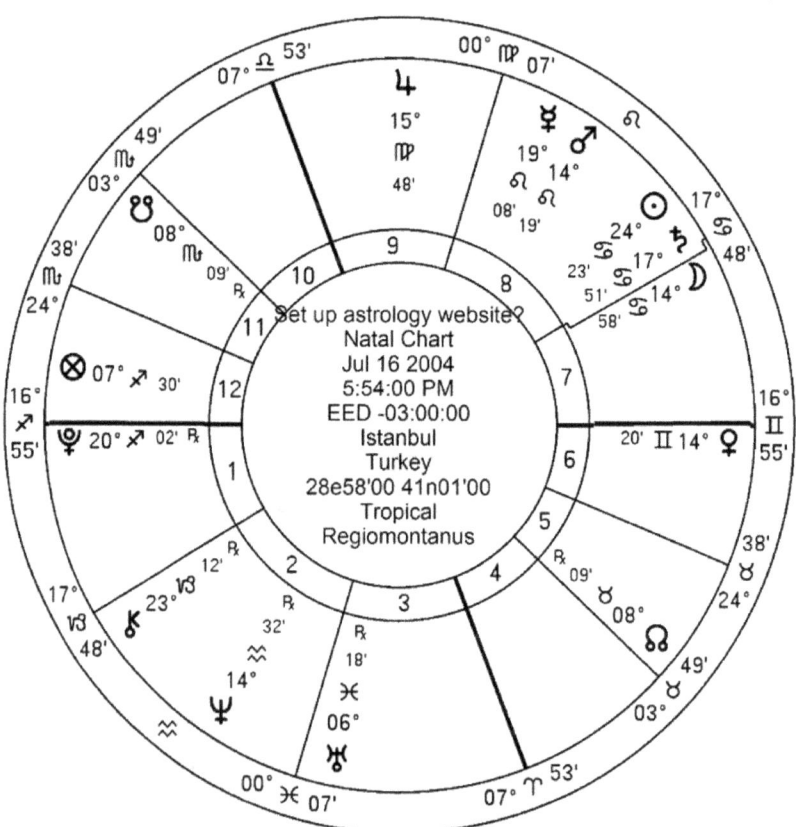

Figure 22: Will we set up the astrology website? What are the problems?

Jupiter, representing the querent as the lord of the Ascendant, was in the 9th and in detriment in Virgo. This indicated the querent's capacity to manage the course of the events was low. In fact, when I asked the question it was not only about me, it was also about all of my friends on that team: so the question was not just about me, it was about "us." Jupiter's position in the 9th showed that the subject of the question was media and publishing, and also astrology. Venus, the lord of the Midheaven, was extremely close to the cusp of the 7th house, representing partnership and joint enterprises. However, she was in a square with Jupiter, the significator of the querent. This indicated that the endeavor would not serve the career and prestige of the querent. The Venus-Pluto opposition also showed that the endeavor would create stress later or change into another form.

When I looked at Jupiter's aspects, I saw he had a sextile with Saturn in the 8th and was applying to a square with Pluto on the Ascendant. Venus, the lord of the Midheaven, was in a mutable sign and peregrine in Gemini, and the Ascendant and lord of the Ascendant were in mutable signs. All those placements in mutable signs showed me that this endeavor would change into another thing than was originally planned.

The Moon, indicating the general course of the events, was placed at the cusp of the 8th house in Cancer and in conjunction with the fixed star Sirius. This position alone would signify that the endeavor would bring more success than expected. However, the Moon was waning and would conjoin Saturn, which was in detriment in Cancer, after 3°.

Many factors were against this endeavor, but what was the reason for that? Why, and because of whom, would this endeavor not work? Interestingly, the 8th house was occupied by many planets. Saturn stood like a barrier in front of the Moon at the cusp of the 8th. Who or what was represented by Saturn then? As the lord of the 2nd house by sign and the exalted lord of the 10th of this chart, the problem would stem from financial matters and/or due to authority figures. Those significations showed that the delay or restriction of the endeavor was due to disagreements on financial matters between the people in charge of this effort.

The South Node, placed in the 11th house, might also give information about the reason for the problem. It might show that the friends who share the same ideals would have some problems. The lord of the 11th, Mars, was in an opposition with Neptune which would soon be exact. This position could be interpreted as meaning that we would have some disappointments within the group of friends or some dubious conditions would occur.

As Jupiter, the lord of the Ascendant, was applying to a square with Pluto, the project was stopped and the discussion ended.

"Will he pull the rug out from under me?"

The querent was working in a managerial position at an international company (see Figure 23). He was an idealist, visionary, and a successful manager who was courageous enough to take the necessary steps for the future of its company. The CEO of the company was uncomfortable with the querent's success, as his position was put in danger. So, he was doing everything to show the querent to be an unsuccessful employee and get rid of him. My client was so anxious about the course of the events he asked me: "Will he pull the rug out from under me?"

Aquarius was rising at the time of the question. Neptune close to the Ascendant indicated that the querent was an idealistic person. As Neptune was about to have some negative aspects, I realized that his anxiety was not for nothing. As Neptune was 2.5° from the Ascendant, I thought he would experience some dissolution after 2.5 months and be ousted.

The most significant thing in the chart was the extremely crowded 12th house. These alignments showed that there were some behind-the-scenes events. The Sun in the 12th showed that his boss was one of the people who was maneuvering in this way. There were two other planets close to the Sun: Venus and Mercury. Venus was retrograding and burned, so I told my client that a woman who was close to the CEO would be a part of the intrigue and would act subversively and support the CEO. The querent confirmed this and told me that the woman was the executive assistant, whom he guessed had had an affair with the CEO. Mercury was also in the 12th house, so there would a third person who was in charge of sending my client out of the company. This would be a male figure (Mercury) or a person who is in charge of communications (Mercury). My client could not guess who this person would be. Later on, he realized that this person was the Human Resources Manager.

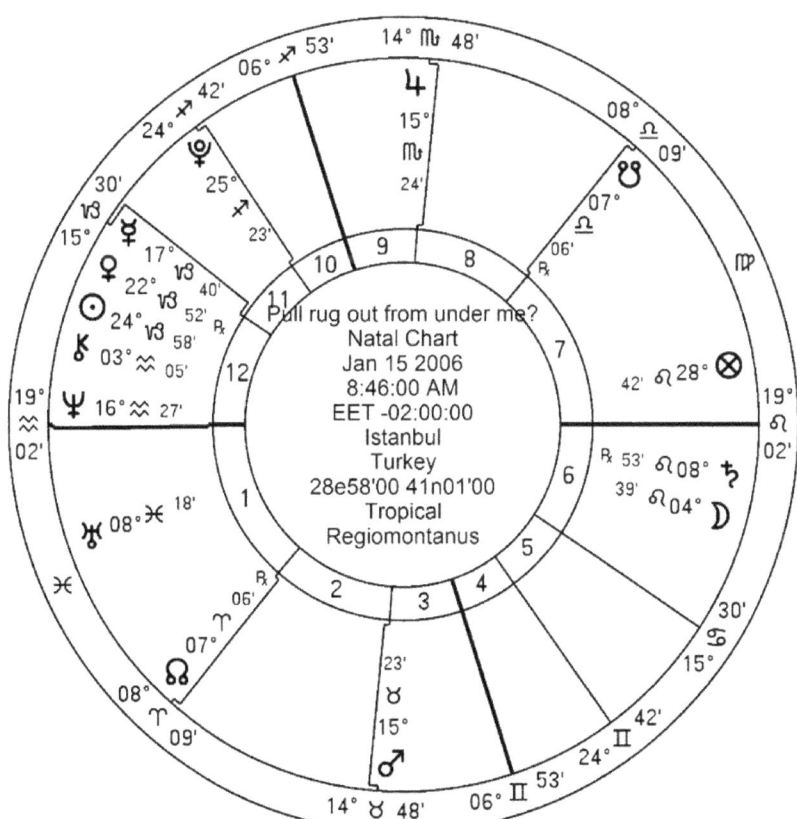

Figure 23: Will he pull the rug out from under me?

Saturn, representing the querent as the lord of the Ascendant, was in the 6th house, in Leo, where he is afflicted and retrograde. This suggested that the querent would not be strong enough to overcome those difficulties, he would not get the support of his underlings, and his working conditions and place of work would undergo a change.

As Saturn (the lord of the Ascendant) and the Moon (the significator of the course of events) were in fixed signs, we might conclude that he would stay in his position. However, as the Sun (the lord of these two significators) was in a cardinal sign and in the 12th, it was obvious that the querent would not stay at his current position. The Moon was about to make an exact conjunction with Saturn within 4°. So, I concluded that the conditions would develop in a negative direction after 4 months.

Another significant aspect in the horary chart was the Grand Cross in fixed signs between Neptune, Jupiter, Saturn, and Mars. The Moon, who was placed in the 5th degree of Leo, was going to activate this hard aspect through conjunctions, squares, and oppositions with the element of the Grand Cross. The intrigues for pulling the rug out from under the querent were seen in the sky.

In a horary chart the top management, managers, and bosses are shown by the 10th house and the Sun. The Sun in the 12th house obviously represented the CEO who was in charge of getting rid of the querent. So, Jupiter (the lord of the 10th house) would be used as the significator for the querent's career and future. Jupiter in the 9th might indicate that the querent would continue his career in far distant places because Sagittarius at the cusp of the 10th house indicates foreigners in general. Mars (the lord of the 9th) and Jupiter (the lord of the Midheaven) being in opposition also showed that the querent would be sent to another position abroad. As this aspect was about to reach the exact degree (only after 0° 02'), the querent would be sent abroad within a very short time. This was what happened! Two and-a-half months after his question, my client was told that he was assigned to another position abroad. This was what Neptune represented by being placed 2.5° from the Ascendant. They pulled the rug out from under him!

My client went abroad where he was assigned, but he was not alone. The CEO who sent him there (who was also a foreigner), was dismissed and sent back to his own country. The female assistant and the manager responsible for human resources were also dismissed. Everyone who was involved in this operation was fired, instead of my client, who was sent to a managerial position abroad. My client is still working abroad in a managerial position and he is very successful at his work.

"Where is the car key?"

The querent was one of my students (see Figure 24). She was very anxious when she called me because her son was going on a trip to Ankara in order to take a school exam but he could not find his car key. He did not buy a bus ticket, as he had planned to go there by car. They searched everywhere in the house but they could not find it and began to panic. They did not have a spare key and, as it was a card key, it was very expensive and they would have to wait a long time for a new key from the car company which was located in Germany. The other reason why they were so anxious was the father of the family: they knew the father would be very angry if they could not find the key. As my student was attending a horary course at our school, she thought she could ask me. She called me and asked: "Where is the car key?"

When I erected the chart, Scorpio was rising. Scorpio is related to secret and mysterious things. It also represents hidden things. So the first thing I wondered was if the key was hidden by someone.

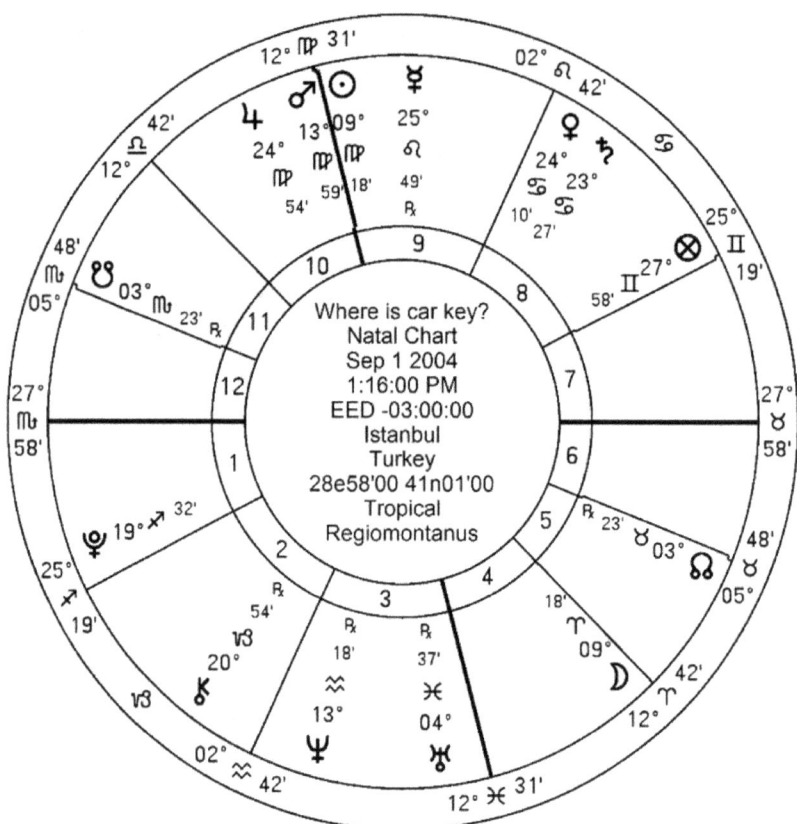

Figure 24: Where is the car key?

The lord of the Ascendant, Mars, was in Virgo in the 10th. As the question was about a lost item, I wanted to use the lord of the Ascendant as the significator of the item. So, the first thing I thought was that the key would be at the office or in a place related to work. Jupiter, the lord of the second house (which represented the lost item as a possession), was also in Virgo and in the 10th house, so it became obvious the lost key would be at the office—but my student was not working and she did not have an office. However, her husband was working and had an office. Venus showed her husband as the lord of the 7th house, and she was in Cancer in the 8th; but the Sun as the natural significator of the spouse was again at the cusp of the 10th house in Virgo. Under those significations, the key should be somewhere at her husband's office or in something related to his occupation. The Lot of Fortune was in the 8th house of the chart, the house which represents the finances and possessions of the spouse. So, I was sure about my prediction.

When looking for lost items we should always see the sign and house of the Lot of Fortune. The lord of the Lot tells us where the lost item is and in what condition it is. The Lot of Fortune was in Gemini, so I thought the key would be somewhere where there is a lot of information and communication, books, papers, or documents. Since the lord of the 2nd house, the lord of the Ascendant, and the Sun were all in Virgo, my suspects were supported and I confirmed that the key would be somewhere Mercurial in nature. Offices, bookcases, a briefcase, and document drawers are of the nature of Virgo and Mercury. So when I made the synthesis with the nature of Gemini, I thought that the key would be in the office, bookcase, file cabinet, file drawer, or briefcase of my student's husband.

Mercury, the lord of the Lot of Fortune, was in Leo and in the 9th house. As Mercury was retrograding, I told my student that the key would be found. Mercury did not have any negative aspects, nor was he burned. So, the key would be found and it would not be damaged. The Moon was about to make a positive aspect with Mercury and the Lot of Fortune. As the Moon was fast and in a cardinal sign, things would proceed quickly. The significators in Virgo were in an angular house. Mars (the lord of the Ascendant) and Jupiter (the lord of the 2nd house, the lost item), were also moving forward fast. All those significators showed that the key would be found quickly.

The 9th house where Mercury was placed, represents far places, but when we derive houses beginning from the 7th, then it corresponds to the 3rd house. That shows the short distance trips (3rd) of the spouse (7th), his siblings and neighbors. Her spouse was not on a short trip, he only went to his office. Daily routine is related to the 6th house, but going to the office everyday if the office is too far from the house may be thought as a 3rd house activity. We might think he dropped the key on the way to the office, or at the place that he went to after a short-distance journey from home to office.

I told my students everything I saw. I also emphasized that the key would be hidden somewhere, as Scorpio was rising. Then she called her husband and told him to look for the key in his desk, drawer, and briefcase. First, her husband objected and said "I didn't take the keys," but later he looked around and found the key within a small messenger bag in the drawer of his steel desk. The son of my student took the key from his father's office and went to Ankara to take the exam.

"Is her illness something bad?"

The querent was one of my friends (see Figure 25). The question was about her boyfriend's sister, who was 13 years old. Her family was worried that she was ill and they already had appointments with various doctors.

Gemini was rising at the time of the question. Normally, the Ascendant and its lord represent the querent, but in answering this question I preferred to use it as the significator of the girl who was ill. This practice was used by William Lilly: if the querent lacks a direct relationship to the person in question, then Ascendant and its lord are used for that quaesited person, not for the querent. On the other hand, when answering this question by derived houses, the 3rd house from the 7th house (that is, the 9th) would indicate the sick girl, because she is the sister (3rd) of the boyfriend (7th) of the woman asking (1st).

The Moon was void in course at the time of the question. Some astrologers think that this is not a good thing in a horary chart as it means that the querent or person in question will experience some negative events. Some think that the answer for any questions asked when Moon was void in course is "nothing will happen," as there is no aspect in front of the Moon (and when there is no aspect in front of Moon, the current situation does not change). This always sounds logical to me. But what is important here is the way the question is asked: for example, if we say "nothing will happen" for this question, we would say that the illness is not something bad.

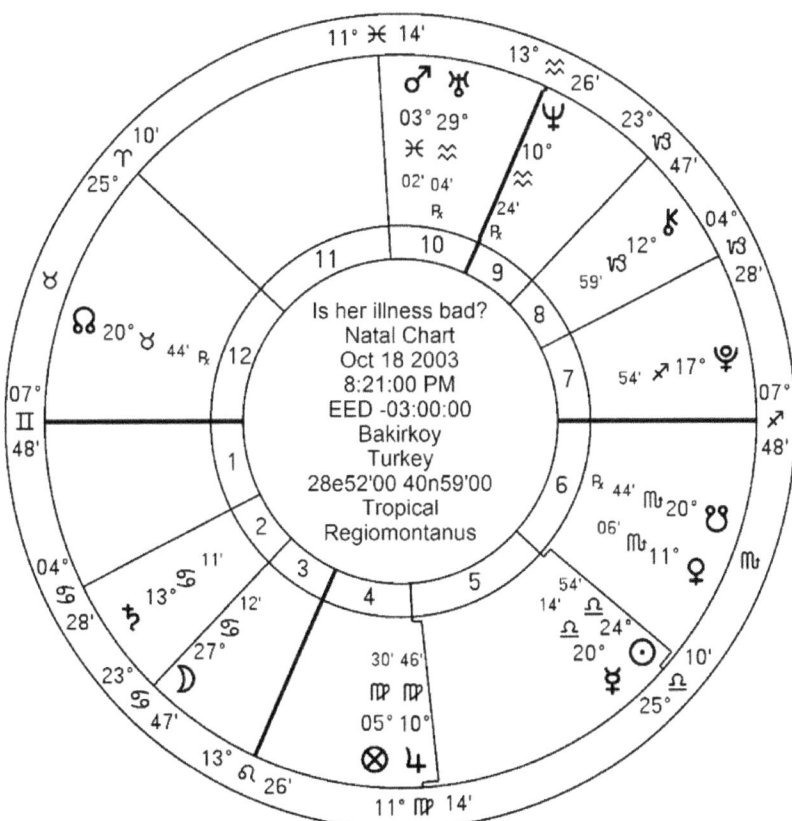

Figure 25: Is her illness something bad?

Since I assigned the Ascendant to the young girl, its lord Mercury was the significator. Mercury was in Libra in a good position in his triplicity, but his strength was lessened because he was in the last degrees of the 5th house and close to the cusp of the 6th. Mercury was also weak because he was burned and applying the Sun; so the girl's health would get worse.

Venus, the lord of the 6th house, was in the 6th; the illness would go further. As Venus was in detriment in Scorpio, we might think that the problem would be related to the lumbar region, kidneys, or ovaries. Venus represents cysts, bumps, benign (or lesser evil) tumors. Venus was about to separate from her square with Neptune and was applying to the South Node: this could be a sign of cancer. I told my friend about this opinion. As Venus was applying to the South Node, the illness was going worse. Moreover, the lord of the 6th house was in her own house, Mercury (the lord of the Ascendant) was not that strong and burned. So the disease would knock the patient down.

The Moon being void in course did not give any information about the course of the events, but her previous aspects pointed out that the conditions were against the patient. The Moon had had an exact square with the afflicted Mercury: this showed that the patient had been experiencing a negative condition. Before being void in course, the Moon had squared the Sun. This indicated the sadness of the young girl's family (the Sun is the lord of the 4th house).

The illness was about to seize the patient; this was very obvious. As the question was "Is her illness something bad?" I examined the 8th house to see if death was close or not. Chiron, which could represent a painful death, was in the 8th. Saturn, the lord of the 8th, was in Cancer in the 2nd house and this position also supported my opinion of a painful death. On the other hand, Mercury and the Moon (the main significators) did not have any applying aspect to Saturn, the lord of the 8th. Venus (representing the illness, as the lord of the 6th) was applying to trine with Saturn (the risk of death as the lord of the 8th). Since this was a positive aspect, the illness would not bring death within a short time. The doctors diagnosed lymphosarcoma. The girl's family did their best for her and sent her to the USA for treatment. The doctors there said she might recover, but the possibility was remote. However, she is still alive and fighting the cancer.

"Is getting divorced the right decision?"

The querent was one of my students who had some problems with her husband and began to think about divorce (see Figure 26). Her husband did not want a divorce. The course of events would be decided by my student, but she was not quite sure about it. She thought she would be rushing into it and asked her question: "Is getting divorced the right decision?" As she also knew astrology, we began to examine the chart together.

Virgo was rising at the time of the question. Mercury, representing the querent (as the lord of the Ascendant), was in Aries (a sign of quick action) in the 8th house: this showed that the querent has jumped to a conclusion. Mercury was also about to go retrograde, showing that the querent was about to give up the idea of separation. Venus, which was very close to the cusp of the 7th house, was about to make a conjunction with Chiron and then with the cusp of the 7th. This symbolized that something would heal this relationship and things would settle.

There was no applying aspect or conjunction between the significator of the querent (Mercury) and the significator of her husband (Jupiter, the lord of the 7th). Mercury was placed in a later degree than Jupiter, separating from him. However, Mercury was going to retrograde the next day and was going to reach Jupiter again. Jupiter was also going direct and applying to Mercury. This signified that this couple would not divorce.

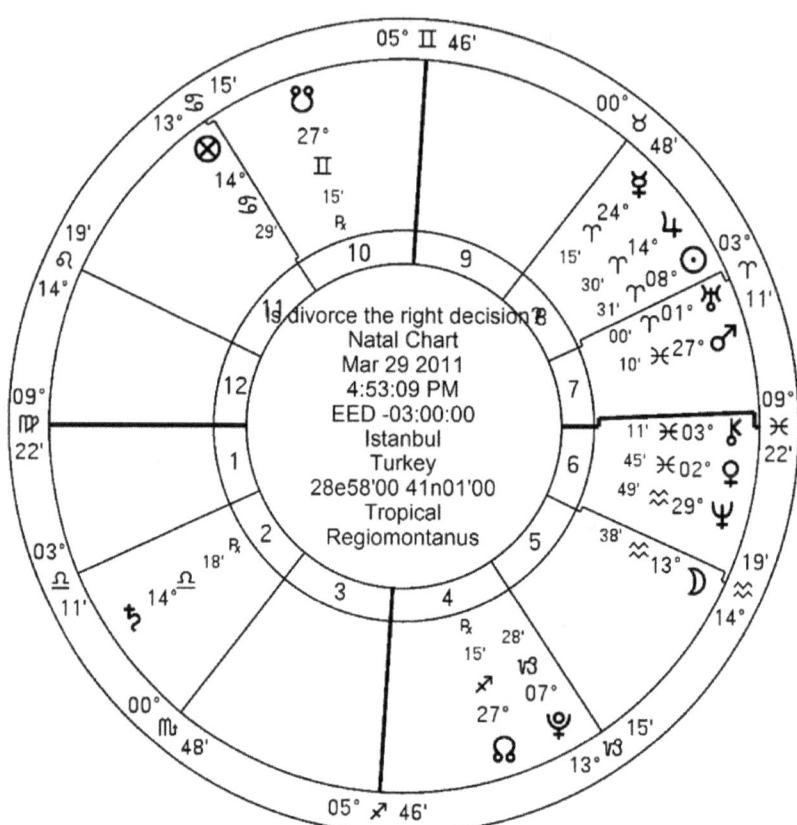

Figure 26: Is getting divorced the right decision?

Moreover, the light would be carried between these two significators: the Moon would make a sextile with Jupiter first and then a sextile with Mercury, so there would be a positive flow between these two significators. As the Moon will bear the light, we might suppose that something or someone else would contribute to this decision. As the Moon ruled the 11th house, a friend of the querent would be helpful. Or, as Moon ruled the 5th from the 7th, the child of the spouse would help…

Jupiter was direct and quick: this showed that the querent's spouse was willing to win her heart and would act quickly. Jupiter was now separating from his opposition with Saturn, so there was no restriction anymore. Saturn ruled the 5th (children) and 6th houses (illness) of the horary chart. The couple wanted to have a baby but it was impossible. The spouse of the querent decided to do all he could do to preserve this marriage, so he made an attempt (Jupiter in Aries, direct and quick) to adopt a baby. Adopting a baby or child is represented by the 11th house (since it is the 5th from the 7th, the children of other people). Again the Moon, the lord of the 11th, carried the light between the main significators (Mercury and Jupiter). This explained that a child would step in and make this relationship work. This child's presence was miraculous: she changed the couple's view of life and their relationship forever. Now they are a family of three and are extremely happy!

"Shall we break up?"

The querent was a television series actress. Her relationship with her boyfriend was not good and she felt they were about to break up. So she asked me: "Is there separation in my chart?" Both the horary chart and her natal chart proved that the querent' feelings were right (see Figure 27).

Pisces was rising at the time of the question, showing that the querent also had the energy to go with the flow. However, as Moon was in Aries, it showed the need to take the initiative and make a decision. The Moon was moving fast, so the events would develop quickly. Mercury, representing the quaesited as the lord of the 7th, was placed in the 7th house. This showed that the question was about the relationship and so it was radical.[137] Mercury was separating from being burned and there was no aspect in front of him: he was void in course. Mercury had had a trine with Mars before his conjunction with the Sun, and before that a square with Pluto. Those aspects represented the recent stress in the relationship.

---

[137] **BD**: One might also say that the lord of the Ascendant (Jupiter) being in the 7th is another indication of radicality.

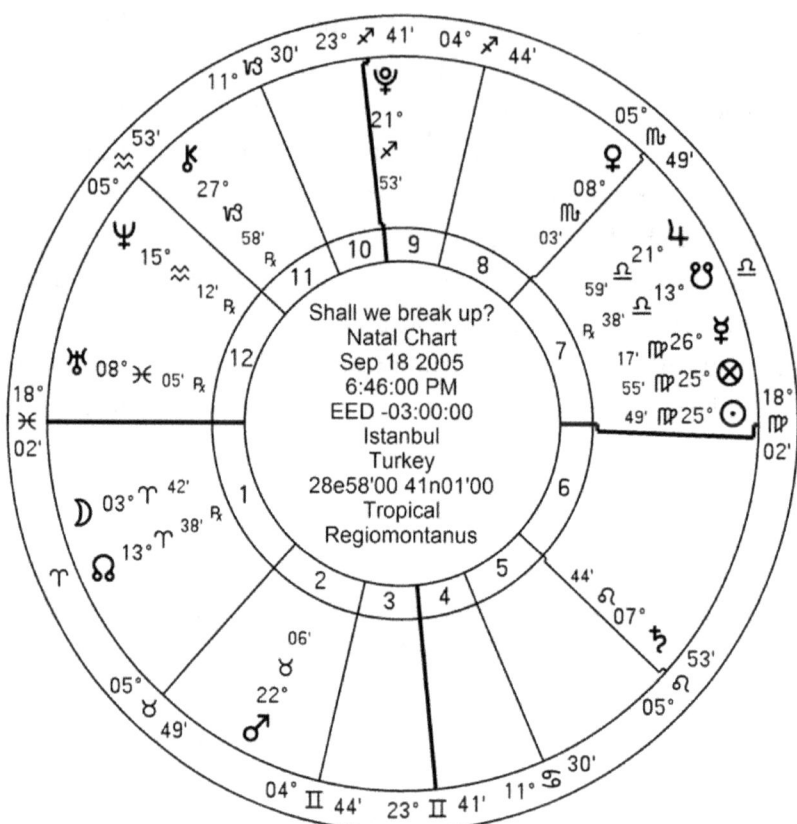

Figure 27: Shall we break up?

Venus, the natural significator of relationships, was in Scorpio where she was in detriment, and in the 8th, which is a stressed house. This position indicated that the relationship was at a critical point. Venus has just separated from her square with Saturn. This showed that the relationship had had some stress lately and this put pressure on both parties. Venus was applying to Uranus in the 12th house, which reflected the need for liberation and getting rid of burdens. Venus's next aspect was first a square with Neptune, and then an opposition with Mars. Those aspects represented dissatisfaction with the relationship (Venus-Neptune square) and disengagement (Venus-Mars opposition). The couple would together decide to break up. The most recent aspect of Moon was an opposition with Jupiter, the lord of the Ascendant. The relationship was about to end.

The couple broke up on the last day of the year (December 31, 2005). When I projected the chart of the day onto the querent's natal chart, I saw that transiting Saturn had an exact square with her natal Mars. On the morning of that day, a New Moon appeared in the natal 12th house and in Capricorn, representing loss and separation. The transiting Venus-Chiron conjunction, representing being wounded in relationships, was on the same degree as the querent's natal ascending degree. Venus retrograding in Aquarius was also pointing out the problems were felt for a long time.

"What will happen to our marriage?"

The querent was one of my previous clients. He had some turmoil in his relationship with his wife and they had been living apart for the last few months. They had a child from their long marriage. Due to the financial crisis my client was experiencing he was working a lot, and as he was so busy with his business he did not have enough time to spend with his wife and child. That's why his wife wanted a divorce. As she was going to take care of their child, she asked for a huge allowance. She thought he should pay both morally and materially for neglecting his wife and child. The couple worked in the same industry, but the financial burden was on the shoulders of my client. For him, his career was important, but he claimed what he had been doing was for the sake of his family and to meet their needs. However, he accepted that he was neglecting them. Due to the condition he was in, he was under stress and highly depressed. So he asked; "What will happen to our marriage?" (see Figure 28).

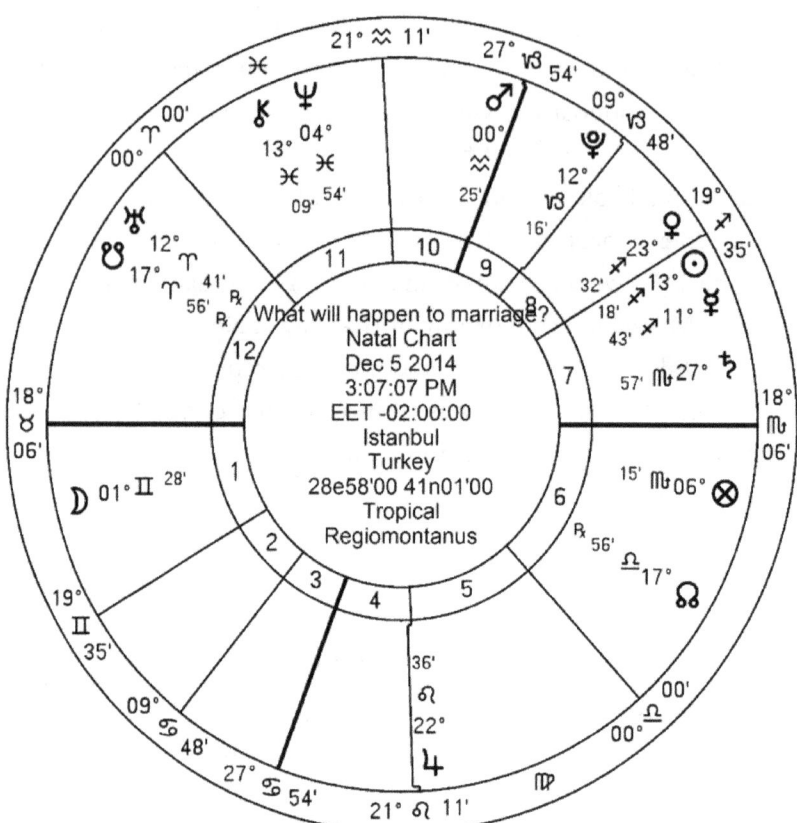

Figure 28: What will happen to our marriage?

Taurus was rising at the time of the question. The querent was also natally a Taurus: his natal Taurus Sun was in his 2nd house, showing financial security was important to him. This was also seen in the chart of the question. He wanted financial security for his family. While he met his family's financial needs in the best way he could, he was not sufficiently connected on an emotional level. Venus, representing the querent (as the lord of the Ascendant) was in the 8th house of the chart. This placement showed that his question was concerned about the huge payment he would have to pay to his wife. His wife demanded a really huge amount of money and she did not retreat one step from her demand. Saturn placed in Scorpio and in the 7th house displayed the attitude of his wife. I told my client, "She looks so cool-headed and tone-deaf. It seems as though she wanted to punish you and take revenge for being neglected. She will not take any step back, I think." My client told me that I was totally right, this was how his wife reacted.

My client's wife had another idea behind her demand. She wanted to set up her own business and realize her dreams with the help of the money she had asked for from her husband. If my client supported her with this cash payment, she would give up asking for monthly payments. Mars, the lord of the 7th, was the significator of the spouse and was in the 10th house of the chart, in Aquarius. The wife had some ideas and wanted to be successful. Venus was in the 8th house, and also the Sun and Mercury were very close to the cusp of that house. I told my client that he would have to make a huge payment (due to the planets in the 8th), his marriage was about to end, and his wife would not give up (Saturn in the 7th and in a fixed sign). My client was also aware of that condition.

The Saturn of the question chart was transiting in my clients natal 8th house: this also showed that he would make payments and would have difficulties in earning money. This was what he was anxious about. He told me, "If I pay her the money she wanted, then I will have very little money left for my own business. If I cannot collect the money for my projects from my clients, I may have to stop doing business." He was stuck in a difficult situation and it was obvious that he could not provide the funds he needed. I told him that these difficulties would continue until the end of 2015. There were some supportive transits, but they were not strong enough to maintain his business.

My client told that he would make this payment to his wife for the future of their child, as his child was very important for him. Jupiter, the lord of the 8th house of the question, was placed in the 5th house, benefiting my client's child. So, he made the payment.

"Will my dog recover?"

The querent's dog was old and all of the vets he took it to said the dog was about to depart this life (see Figure 29). Those were the last days of his little pet, perhaps. He knew what was going to happen, but he asked me, "Shall my dog recover?"

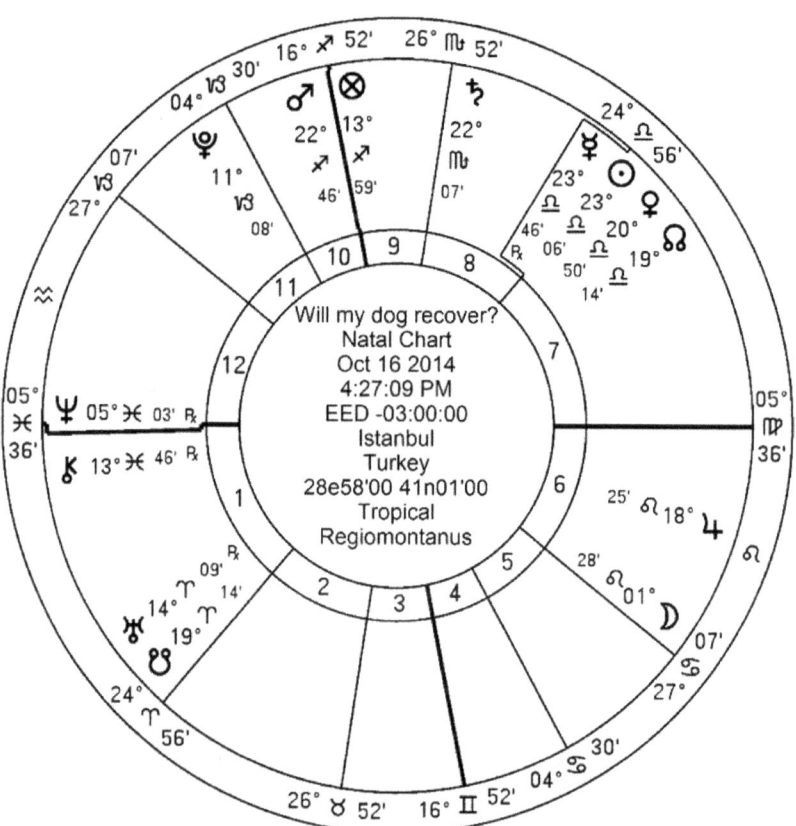

Figure 29: Will my dog recover?

Neptune rising at the horizon represented the grief of the querent and also that he accepted that it was time for the dog to pass away, despite asking such a question. Chiron placed in the 1st showed that the question was asked with a hope for recovery but there was an emotional pain here.

As the question is about the dog, we should look at the 6th house. The chart was radical as the Moon was in the 6th house. On the other hand, Moon was peregrine in Leo. In fact, this was a good position for the health of the dog; we might also say the same thing for Jupiter in Leo in the 6th house, because Jupiter was the exalted lord of the 6th house and also a benefic planet. The Moon applying to Jupiter was a good signification, indicating the dog would recover. However, after a conjunction with Jupiter and sextile with Venus, the Moon would apply to a square with Saturn who was placed at the end of the 8th house and close to the cusp of the 9th. Saturn being the victor of the 8th house represented death. Moreover, the Sun (who was the lord of the Moon and Jupiter) was at the cusp the 8th house and in Libra, where he was afflicted by being in fall.

I told the querent that his dog would first recover but then pass away. The doctors predicted that the dog would not live more than one month. As the Moon-Saturn square would be exact after 21°, I predicted that the dog would only live 21 days more. The dog died after 28 days, on November 13, 2014, when the Moon and Jupiter had a conjunction in Leo. The querent's only prayer was for a painless death for his dog, and this became true. The Moon-Jupiter conjunction in the chart of the question was repeated on the day of the dog's last day, and the dog passed away without any pain.

"Will I be the distributor?"

The querent was a businessman and the distributor of some foreign brands in Turkey (see Figure 30). He was in contact with a new company and he wanted to apply to be their distributor but he was not quite sure about it. So he asked his question, "Will I be the distributor?"

The first degrees of Scorpio were rising at the time of the question. This suggested that it was too early to make a decision about the question, there would be some conditions that the querent did not know about, and the situation was not clear yet.

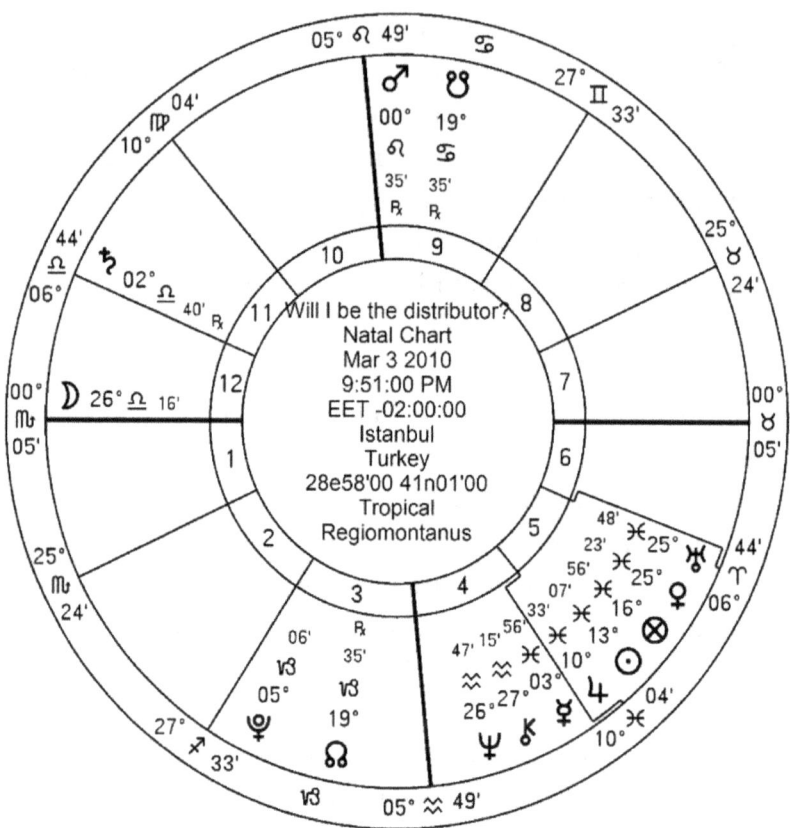

Figure 30: Will I be the distributor?

The Moon was in the burned path (or *via combusta*) in the 12th house, in Libra. This showed that getting the distributorship would not be a good idea, the querent might suffer from the partnership, and some out-of-control events would be possible.

Mars, the significator of the querent (as the lord of the Ascendant), was in the 9th house (foreigners and foreign lands) and peregrine in the first degree of Leo, and retrograding. It seemed he would give up on getting this distributorship, which he was not sure about already. The South Node was also in the 9th, showing that he would not be able to get good results from business with foreigners. We may expect some losses, intrigues, and speculations related to where the South Node is placed. So, although business partnership was related to foreigners and foreign countries and it looked attractive, it would bring some damage to the querent.

As the question was related to business, I had to look at the 10th house; and as it was connected with distributorship, I also had to look at the 7th house (partnership, one-to-one relationships, distributorship) and also the 8th house (money earned from this partnership).

The Sun, the lord of the 10th house, was peregrine in Pisces. This signified that the business would not be very attractive. The Sun has just separated from Jupiter and was applying to the Lot of Fortune, showing that the brand was a prestigious one and partnership with such a brand would bring profit. However, the most significant thing in the chart was not how prestigious that brand was, but rather that the parties would not be able to get along and there would be some problems in the partnership. Venus, the lord of the 7th and 8th houses, was in Pisces where she was exalted, but she was about to conjoin with Uranus within a short time. This showed there would be some changes in the conditions and an unexpected decision to give up this partnership. That was the case. The querent gave up getting this distributorship. He had a meeting with the representatives of the brand as the meeting was already scheduled, but the parties could not agree on the working conditions and they did not shake hands.

"Is he the one I will marry?"

The querent was a woman who has been my client for a long time and who was willing to marry (see Figure 31). She was highly interested in spiritual studies and she was influenced by a man whom she had met in a spiritual practice group. The man was friendly but distant; however, my client asked her question: "Is he the one that I will marry?"

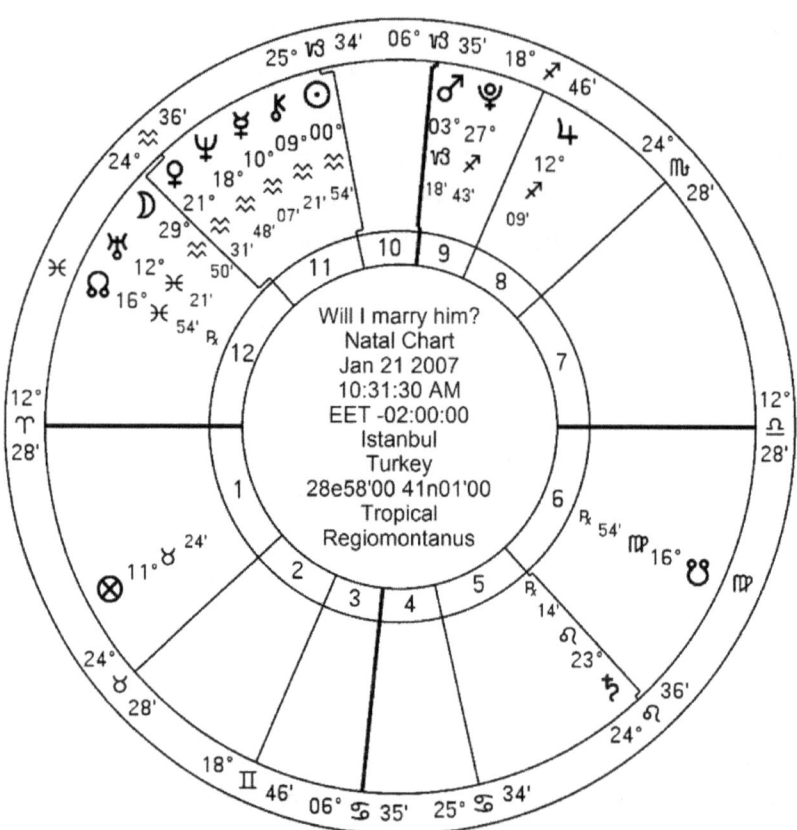

Figure 31: Is he the one I will marry?

Aries, the sign related to decisiveness, action, initiative, and also impetuosity, was rising. Mars, representing the querent as the lord of the Ascendant, was in Capricorn in the 9th house, very close to the cusp of the 10th. The querent was looking for a reliable, sound, and prestigious partner with whom she would be able to organize her life, and this approach was obvious in the horary chart.

Venus, representing the man whom the querent had asked the question about, was peregrine in Aquarius and in the 12th house. This placement did not mean marriage. There was no applying aspect between the lord of the Ascendant and the lord of the 7th, and the Moon did not carry the light between them. A third planet which is slower than these two also did not collect their light. The Moon and Venus were not applying to each other. All those factors showed that this man was not the one whom my client would marry. Venus separating from Neptune signified that this could be an idealized or platonic relationship, but was going to make an opposition with Saturn. That was an indicator that there would be no relationship at all between these two people. My client met this man at some other spiritual events but they only said "hello" to each other.

"Will this project be a success? Will I get my money?"

The querent was a woman teaching handicrafts (see Figure 32). She was working as a consultant for a company which marketed visual and printed education kits about handicrafts. It was a unique project when it was first planned: they aimed at training for the disabled and prisoners, however things did not go well. Project managers were changed continuously and the project did not display any stability. The querent could not get her money from the company and so she asked: "Will this project continue? Will it be successful? Shall I get my money?"

Leo, which represents creativity, recognition, being on stage, and the will of success, was rising at the time of the question. The querent's natal Ascendant was also in Leo and her natal Sun was in a strong place. In the chart of the question, the Sun or lord of the Ascendant was in the 11th house and was peregrine in Gemini. This indicated that the project would bring recognition to the querent. The Sun was peregrine in Gemini, but as Mercury, being the lord of

Gemini, was also in the same sign, it strengthened the Sun. This showed that the profit would come through communication skills. She had already received some of her money, but as the project did not show any progress she thought she would not get the rest. The Sun, Moon, and Mercury were all placed in Gemini, a sign related to teaching, the transfer of information, marketing, and publicity. Although a lot of money was spent on the publicity and marketing of this project, the desired result had not been achieved.

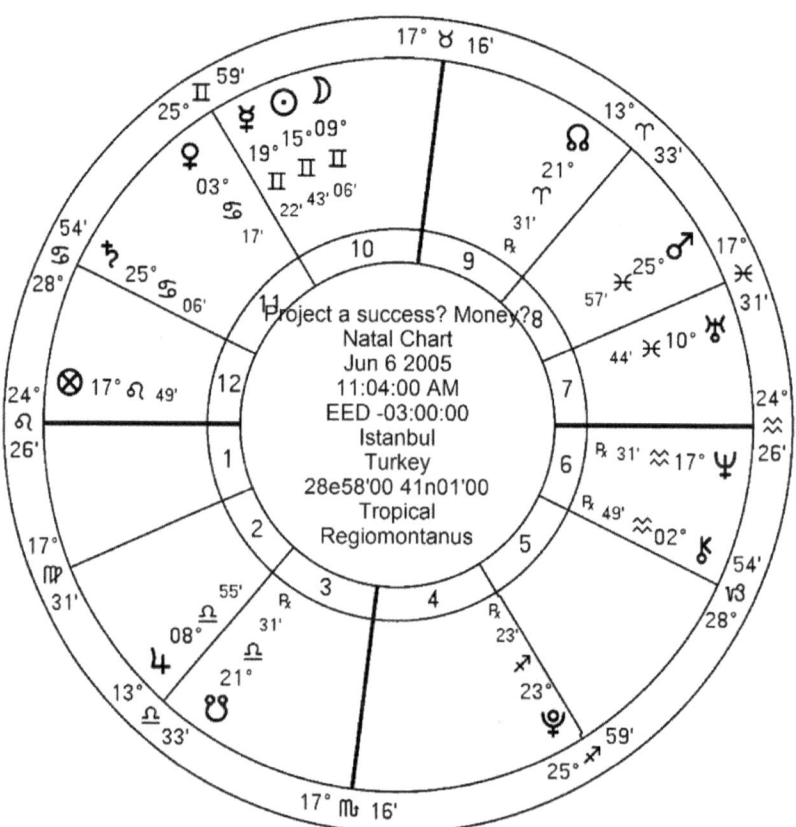

**Figure 32: Will this project be a success?
Will I get my money?**

The Moon was waning at the time of the question; this position showed that the project was about come to an end. The waning Moon also symbolized that the energy was decreasing and something would be released.

Three significators were in a strong position in the 10th house of the chart. However, they were in the opposition of Pluto, who was at the cusp of the 5th house and retrograding in Sagittarius. This indicated that the project would not show the desired progress, and there would be some separations and power struggles. The Sun, who was one of those significators and represented the querent, was going to reach the exact opposition of Pluto after 8°. So the querent would probably quit this job (the waning Moon) after 8 weeks or 8 months, or there would be some struggles (Sun-Pluto opposition) as she could not get her money.

Mercury, being the lord of the 2nd and 11th houses, represented the money of the querent and the profit that would come from that business. As the Mercury-Pluto opposition would reach exactness after 4°, the possibility for getting her money would decrease after 4 weeks or 4 months. Mercury's next aspect was with Mars, who is in the 8th house (which represents the money owed to the querent), showing she would not be able to get her money.

The Moon, the fastest of the three planets placed in the 10th house and the planet which represents the course of events, will first make a square with Uranus in the 7th house and then a conjunction with the Sun (being burned), then a conjunction with Mercury, and finally will trigger the Pluto-Mars square.

All of these aspects showed that things would get difficult; there would be some sudden and unexpected developments, some problems between the project managers and the partner, and some financial problems. So, I told the querent that this project would not be efficient enough, would not bring the expected profit, some of the partners would quit, and due to financial problems and disagreement she would not be able to get the rest of her money. I also added that this project would bring her prestige anyway. The project was completed, and did not bring the expected results. After a while, the partners separated. The project could not be managed properly and some tools of the project were sold separately. And unfortunately, the querent could not get her remaining money. Although the project did bring her recognition and prestige, she did not take part in other projects of that company.

Appendix A: Table of Dignities

Appendix B: Glossary

Accidental Benefic: A malefic planet located in one of the benefic houses; in dignity and not afflicted; bringing limited benefit but no affliction at all.

Accidental Dignity: The strength a planet gains for some reason other than its zodiacal position. Planets located in the angular houses fulfill 100% of their promises; planets located in the succedent houses fulfill 50% of their promises, and planets in the cadent houses fulfill 25% of their promises.

Accidental Malefic: A benefic planet located in one of the malefic houses; in detriment, fall or afflicted; bringing affliction more than benefits.

Afflicted; Impeded: An indicator of weakness. It means being restricted, disabled and ill. Afflicted planets cannot fulfill their promises. States that afflict the planets are described in detail in Bonatti's *146 Considerations*. The most important afflictions are being located in cadent houses, being burned, retrograde, and being in conjunction, square, or opposition with malefics without reception.

Alcocoden: See **House-master**.

Alien: A planet having no essential dignities. Often called "peregrine." Such a planet is similar to a foreigner who travels in a foreign country and who has no rights or no business there. Its state in this position is linked with the ruler of this place.

Almutem Figuris: See **Victor of the chart**.

Almuten: See **Victor**.

Analogy: The similarity/ parallelism of the nature of the planets with the houses and signs they are in.

Anaretic: Derived from Greek; refers to a point that is fatal and destroying in primary directions.

Angles: The main structural keys of the chart, which give the primary house themes and planetary strength. Planets located in the angular houses have stronger and more visible impacts.

Angular Houses: see **Cardinal Houses.**

Aphelion: The point in the orbit of a planet where it is farthest from the Sun.

Aphetic: Refers to places which are suitable for the longevity **releaser** or "hyleg" to be in.

Arabic Parts: See **Lots.**

Ascendant: The degree of the zodiac which crosses the eastern horizon, and in quadrant house systems the cusp of the 1st house. The sign to which this degree belongs, is the "rising sign."

Aspects: From words that mean "to look at," configurations between two places in the zodiac which give information about how planets especially express their influences. on how the planets express their influences. The six "Ptolemaic" aspects are at intervals of 60°, 90°, 120°, and 180°. The conjunction is usually included among these, although it is not an aspect.

Bad Houses: 6th, 8th, and 12th houses.

Bad Placement: Being placed in its detriment or fall, being cadent, or being in a conjunction or aspect with malefics.

Badly Disposed: Being placed in a weak house and being not dignified. Having incompatible aspects and no contact with its ruler also makes a planet badly disposed.

Being in dignity: A planet which has at least one of the major dignities (domicile, exaltation, triplicity, term and face rulerships) is in dignity. The most powerful dignities are domicile and exaltation rulerships.

Benefics, Benefic Planets: Benefics are planets that assist the native in a positive outcome without making too much effort, bring benefits, support, and balance him in a moderate way. Benefic planets are Jupiter, Venus and the Sun. The waxing Moon and in some cases Mercury may also be considered benefics.

Besieged, Enclosure: A planet which lies between two planets (especially the malefics). A planet may be besieged through a conjunction or an aspect.

Burned: A planet which is 8.5° close to the Sun. A burned planet is afflicted. It is one of the debilities. According to ancient astrologers, it is the most serious debility.

Cadent Houses: 3rd, 6th, 9th, and 12th houses.

Cardinal Houses: 1st, 4th, 7th, and 10th houses. Also known as angular houses.

Cazimi: When a planet is within the 17' of the Sun, it is cazimi. A cazimi planet is "in the heart of the Sun" and so it is under some kind of divine protection as it is so close to the Sun's spirit.

Combust: See **Burned.**

Debility, debilitated: A planet located in the sign of its detriment or fall, where a planet is in the sign opposite the sign it rules (detriment) or is exalted (fall). Such planets cannot fulfill their promises. Malefics so debilitated cause trouble, so their malefic impacts increase. According to some astrologers, being placed in a weak house, having hard aspects with the malefics, being retrograde, and being burned are also debilities.

Declination: The angular distance of a planet north or south of the celestial equator.

Derived Houses: Houses counted from other places or houses, in order to see the chart from a broader perspective. For example, the 2nd natal house indicates the native's money; but because the 5th house is the 2nd from the 4th (indicating the father), the 5th house also indicates the father's money in addition to its normal signification for children.

Dignity: The strength, advantage, or virtue of a planet. This word is also used to describe the various types of rulerships a planet has.

Dispositor: A planet which rules the sign that another planet is located in. For example, if Venus is in Aries, she is disposed by Mars.

Diurnal Planets: Sun, Jupiter, and Saturn.

Domicile Rulership: If a planet is placed in a house that it rules, it feels as if it is at its own home. It displays its nature comfortably and fulfills its promises. For example, the Moon is the domicile ruler of Cancer.

Double-Bodied Signs: The mutable signs, which are Gemini, Virgo, Sagittarius, and Pisces.

Descendant: The point opposite the **Ascendant**, where the zodiac crosses the western horizon.

Duodecimae: See **Twelfth-parts.**

Eastern: Planets which rise before the Sun. Planets which are eastern of the Sun are powerful; they may fulfill their promises efficiently; acceptable and praiseworthy. According to the rules of medieval astrology, Mercury and Venus are eastern when they rise after the Sun.

Eastern Quarters: The quarters of the chart between the ASC-MC and DSC-IC.

Ecliptic: The plane defined by the Sun's motion, which the zodiac is centered on.

Electional Astrology: The branch of astrology used for choosing the right time for actions, often consulted for business ventures, surgical operations, signing agreements, buying and selling, etc.

Elevation; Elevated: A planet which is close to the Midheaven, even if having passed more than 5° beyond it. This placement indicates the things that the native prioritizes.

Essential Dignity: A dignity which a planet has through the zodiac (such as being in the sign of its exaltation). A planet located in one of these dignities have the power to fulfill its promises, but domicile and exaltation rulership are strongest.

Exaltation Rulership: A planet in its own exaltation is like a person who is near the king, who is respected and rewarded. Having exaltation rulership lets the nature of the planet be manifested plainly. For example: the Sun is the exalted ruler of Aries, and when in it he is "exalted."

Face: Each 10° of the zodiac: each sign has three faces, with 36 total in the zodiac. Each face is ruled by a planet: for example, the second face lord of Gemini is Mars. Although face rulership brings the least dignity, it is important anyway.

Feminine Planets: Moon, Venus, and sometimes Mercury

Final Dispositor: A final dispositor is a planet which all other planets are ultimately dependent on because it is the only one in its own sign of the zodiac (like the Sun in Leo).

Fixed Stars: Fixed stars for the constellations. Unlike the planets, fixed stars look stationary from the earth; but due to the precession of the equinoxes they move less than 1' per year and 1° every 72 years. Those closest to the ecliptic, and the brightest, have distinguished importance.

Friendly Planets: Planets which are compatible with each other, having the same natures.

Good Houses: Houses except the 6th, 12th, and 8th houses.

Good Placement: Being placed in its dignity or in strong houses, well-aspected and contact with its ruler.

Halb: One of the minor dignities indicating that a planet will be more active and influential. In a diurnal chart, if a diurnal planet is above the horizon (or in a nocturnal chart below the horizon), then it is *halb*. In a nocturnal chart, if a nocturnal planet is above the horizon (or in a diurnal chart below the horizon(, then it is *halb*.

Hayz: From the Arabic word *hayyiz* which means "domain": a minor dignity which is more influential than *halb*. In a diurnal chart, if a diurnal planet is above the horizon (or in a nocturnal chart below the horizon) and in one of the masculine signs, then it is in its *hayz* or domain. Similarly, in a nocturnal chart if a nocturnal planet is above the horizon (or in a diurnal chart below the horizon) and in one of the feminine signs, then it is in its *hayz* or domain.

Horary Astrology: A branch of astrology dealing with questions "of the hour." The astrologer erects the chart for the moment he understands the client's question, and makes a prediction. Horary astrology was widely used because people often did not know their exact birth time.

Hostile Planets: Planets which are incompatible with each other, having opposite natures.

House-master: Derived from a Persian word indicating a planet that grants years in longevity techniques.

Houses: The division of a chart into 12 sections, each of which signifies a particular realm of experience or life. The houses where the planets are located in a chart are important factors in reading.

Hyleg: See **Releaser**.

IC (Imum Coeli): The part of the zodiac passing the lower meridian to the north, and in quadrant houses the cusp of the 4th house. It is opposite the **MC**.

In contact: In aspect or conjunction with something.

Increasing in Light: The process by which the Moon's light increases until it is full.

Intercepted Sign: A sign which has no cusp on it.

Joys: Planets rejoice in the houses which are compatible with their natures and where they may express their natures comfortably. Planets have houses in which they rejoice (such as Venus in the 5th), and also signs (such as Venus in Taurus).

Local Determination: How a planet's general nature is specified to a particular area of life due to the house it is in. This phrase is a technical term in the work of Morin.

Lots: A position derived from the position of three other parts of a chart. Normally, the distance between two places is measured in zodiacal order from one to the other, and this distance is projected forward from some other place (usually the Ascendant): where the counting stops, is the Lot.

Luminaries: The Sun and the Moon.

Lunar Nodes: The points where the Moon intersects the plane of the ecliptic. The *South Node* is where the Moon crosses it into southern latitude, and the *North Node* where she crossed into northern latitude. Traditionally the *North Node* is considered to be equivalent to a benefic, whereas the *South Node* is equivalent to a malefic.

Malefics: A planet which requires a great effort to be productive, which brings trouble and restrictions. They are unproductive and prone to extremism. Planets malefic by nature are Saturn and

Mars. The waning Moon and in some cases Mercury may also be considered as malefics.

Masculine Planets: Sun, Saturn, Jupiter, Mars, and sometimes Mercury.

MC (Medium Coeli), Midheaven: Where the zodiac crosses the southern meridian, and in quadrant houses the cusp of the 10th house.

Minor Dignity: A dignity apart from the usual five essential dignities (for example, **hayz**).

Moiety: One-half of an **orb**, i.e. the number of degrees on either side of a planet or other point, which defines its special range of influence.

Mundane Astrology: The branch of astrology concerned with predictions for political, social, financial, religious, or military events.

Mutual Interaction: see **Mutual Reception**.

Mutual Reception: When two planets are placed in each other's domiciles, they are in mutual reception: they "host" each other. Bonatti suggested that these two planets should aspect each other for a mutual reception. On the other hand, Abū Ma'shar, Ibn Ezra and William Lilly suggested if these two planets are in each other's dignities by domicile, exaltation, or other rulerships, they do not need an aspect to create a mutual interaction: this is called "generosity."

Natal Astrology: The branch of astrology which casts a chart for someone's birth, with techniques for determining the native's personal potentials, tendencies, motivations, accidents that he may experience, financial situation, relationships, and so on.

Nocturnal Planets: Moon, Venus, and Mars.

North Node: See **Lunar Nodes**.

Ninth-parts: A subdivision of each sign into nine parts, each formed of 3° 20'.

Novenaria: See **Ninth-parts**.

Occidental: See **Western**.

Orb. A span of degrees on either side of a body or point, which indicates a range of power. See also **moiety**.

Oriental: See **Eastern**.

Paran: Star or star groups that fall upon angles at the same time that another significant constellation or planet is also upon the angles. They are viewed as attendants. In ancient astrology the term was also applied to the constellations that ascended with the zodiacal decans.

Peregrine: See **Alien**.

Perihelion: The point in the orbit of a planet where it is nearest to the Sun.

Powerful Planet: Refers to a planet's capacity to fulfill the things it represents naturally or accidentally. A powerful planet may have an impact on an end result. The power of a planet is determined through its position in the chart, including its essential and accidental placement and some other factors.

Primary Directions: A method of directions based on primary motion or the diurnal rotation of the heavens.

Quadruplicity: A qualitative division of the signs into three groups, each with four signs. These three groups are called cardinal, fixed and mutable signs. Aries, Cancer, Libra, and Capricorn are cardinal signs; Taurus, Leo, Scorpio, and Aquarius are fixed signs; Gemini, Virgo, Sagittarius, and Pisces are mutable signs.

Reception: When a planet host another planet in the sign which it rules. When two planets are in **mutual reception**, both of them gain power and they act as if they are in their own rulerships.

Releaser: A planet or point directed by **primary directions**, to predict the length of life and other life crises.

Retrograde: When a planet seems to slow down, stop, and turn backwards in the zodiac. It is one of the most important debilities. A retrograde significator is passive and has difficulty in fulfilling its promises.

SAN: See **Syzygy**.

Sect: A division of charts, planets, and signs into "diurnal/day" and "nocturnal/night." Charts are diurnal if the Sun is above the horizon, otherwise they are nocturnal.

Solar Arcs: A predictive technique in which each planet is directed at the same rate in which the Sun is directed in secondary progressions, with 1 year = 1 degree. There is no retrograde motion in this technique because it does not represent the native's psychology (as in progressions).

South Node: See **Lunar Nodes**.

Succedent Houses: Houses which follows the angular houses: the 2nd, 5th, 8th, and 11th.

Syzygy: The pre-natal New or Full Moon degree. The syzygy before birth is used in many natal techniques, such as in predicting longevity or determining the **victor of the chart**.

Terms: A division of each sign into five parts; each term is ruled by a single planet. For example, Venus is the term ruler of Cancer between 7° – 13°. The luminaries do not rule any terms in the three standard sets of terms (which are the Egyptian, Chaldean, and Ptolemaic).

Tolerance: See **Orb**.

Triplicity Lords: A group of three planets ruling over each set of signs in a **triplicity**, divided into the day, night, and partnering rulers. Triplicity lords were used extensively by Dorotheus and later astrologers, to understand the support given to a particular point in the chart.

Triplicity: A classification of the signs into groups of three, by their elements: Fire, Earth, Air and Water signs. Aries, Leo, and Sagittarius are Fire signs; Taurus, Virgo, and Capricorn are Earth signs; Gemini, Libra, and Aquarius are Air signs; Cancer, Scorpio, and Pisces are Water signs.

Twelfth-parts: A division of each sign into twelve parts, each formed of 2° 30'.

Via Combusta ("Burned path"): The area between 15° Libra and 15° Scorpio. Considered to be a debilitating area, especially for the Moon. According to some astrologers like Māshā'allāh and al-Bīrūnī, it is between 19° Libra and 3° Scorpio, which are the degrees of the fall of the luminaries.

Victor: The planet which gets the highest score over one or more positions, according to the table of dignities; the most dignified planet of any specific zodiacal degree.

Victor of the chart: It is the key of the whole chart; the key for the native's life. It represents the force that dominates the native's life. It may also be considered as describing the primary characteristics of the native.

Void of Course: When a planet, especially the Moon, remains out of orb of any aspect (or does not complete an exact aspect) so long as it is in its current sign.

Weak Planet: A planet which has difficulties in fulfilling its natural and accidental promises, and cannot bring a result or cannot impact the final result. Weakness is determined through a planet's essential and accidental placement, along with other factors.

Well disposed: When the lord of the sign in which some planet is located, is in a good **zodiacal state**.

Western: Planets which set after the Sun. Planets which are western of the Sun have difficulty in fulfilling their promises. They have anti-social methods which may be questioned.

Western Quarters: The quarters of the chart between the MC-DSC and IC-ASC.

Whole Signs: The oldest system of assigning house topics. In this system, each sign is a house, so there are no intercepted signs. It was used by many astrologers, sometimes along with quadrant systems (such as Alchabitius semi-arcs, Placidus, etc.).

Zodiac: The belt of twelve signs.

Zodiacal State: A planet's strength (dignity) or weakness, especially in terms of the type of house, sign (dignity), and relationship to its lord.

References

Al-Bīrūnī, *The Book of Instruction in the Elements of the Art of Astrology* (London: Luzac & Co., 1934)

Al-Qabīsī, *The Introduction to Astrology*, eds. Charles Burnett, Keiji Yamamoto, Michio Yano (London and Turin: The Warburg Institute, 2004)

Al-Rijāl, 'Alī ibn Abī, *De Iudiciis Astrorum* (Basel: Henrichus Petrus, 1551)

Appleby, Derek, *Horary Astrology* (Bel Air, MD: Astrology Classics, 2005)

Ayduz, Salim, *Osmanlı Devleti'nde Müneccimbaşılık ve Müneccimbaşılar* (T.C. İstanbul University Social Sciences Institute, Science and History Department Postgraduate Thesis, 1993)

Barclay, Olivia, *Horary Astrology Rediscovered: A Study in Classical Astrology* (Atglen, PA: Whitford Press, 1990)

Bonatti, Guido, *The Book of Astronomy*, Vols. I-II (Golden Valley, MN: The Cazimi Press, 2007)

Dorotheus of Sidon, *Carmen Astrologicum*, trans. and ed. Benjamin N. Dykes (Minneapolis, MN: The Cazimi Press, 2017)

Dykes, Benjamin trans. and ed., *The Book of the Nine Judges* (Minneapolis, MN: The Cazimi Press, 2011)

Ebertin, Reinhold, *The Combination of Stellar Influences* (Tempe, AZ: American Federation of Astrologers, 2004)

Frawley, John, *The Horary Textbook* (London: Apprentice Books, 2005)

Goldstein-Jacobson, Ivy, *Simplified Horary Astrology* (Pasadena, CA: Pasadena Lithographers, 1970)

Green, H.S., Charles E. O. Carter, and Raphael, *Mundane Astrology: The Astrology of Nations and States* (Abingdon, MD: Astrology Classics, 2005)

Houlding, Deborah, *The Houses: Temples of the Sky*, 2nd Edition (Bournemouth, England: The Wessex Astrologer Ltd., 2006)

Houlding, Deborah and Öner Döşer, *Astrology of Questions* [Turkish language only] (Istanbul: AstroArt Astrology School Publishing, March 2015)

Koç, Gulcin Tunali, *Osmanlı Siyaset Kültürünü Anlamada Kaynak Olarak İlm-i Nücum: Sadullah el-Ankaravi* (Bogazici University, Unpublished Postgraduate Thesis, 2002)

Lehman, J. Lee, *The Martial Art of Horary Astrology* (Atglen, PA: Whitford Press, 2002)

Lilly, William, *Christian Astrology* Books I-II (Abingdon, MD: Astrology Classics, 2004)

Louis, Anthony, *Horary Astrology Plain & Simple* (St. Paul, MN: Llewellyn Publications, 1998)

March, Marion D., and Joan McEvers, *The Only Way to Learn About Horary and Electional Astrology* [Volume 6] (San Diego, CA: ACS Publications, 1998)

Māshā'allāh, *On Reception*, in Benjamin Dykes trans. and ed., *Works of Sahl & Māshā'allāh* (Golden Valley, MN: The Cazimi Press, 2008)

Ward, Sue, *The Considerations Before Judgment* [*Considerations*], 1995 (online at http://www.horary.com/sward/Consids.html)

Ward, Sue, *The Traditional Horary Course: Foundation Course* (Privately issued, 2002)

Watters, Barbara H., *Horary Astrology and the Judgment of Events* (Washington, DC: Valhalla Paperbacks, Ltd., 1973)

About the AstroArt Astrology School

Since its establishment in 2005, the AstroArt Astrology School aims at bringing sound and qualified astrological knowledge to society. In the constant pursuit of this goal over the past 13 years, it has succeeded in distinguishing itself and has been a pioneer in many areas, providing high standards of astrological education and creating a lively astrological community in Turkey.

The popularity of AstroArt derives mainly from our ability to offer a graded educational curriculum, covering both traditional and modern astrological techniques. We also offer many different specialty classes for those wishing to improve their knowledge after completing the certificate course. Our specialty courses cover a wide range of topics, namely: medical astrology, financial astrology, mundane astrology, esoteric astrology, Uranian astrology, cosmic astrology, horary astrology, and electional astrology. These classes are run by 11 different tutors who are expert in their chosen subjects.

We have also widened our teaching group with international lecturers, including Glenn Perry on astro-psychology and Aleksandar Imsiragic on Hermetic astrology. Gaye Döşer also presents on cosmic astrology and healing. We have also expanded our esoteric astrology studies by applying Islamic mysticism (Sufism) to astrology.

We are proud to have created many ways of providing knowledge on a country-wide basis: our online interactive classes and our web broadcasts through Astrology TV derive from this mission. So far we reach Germany, Holland, and Cyprus, as well as many other cities, by which we have brought a solid education to those who are physically unable to attend the school.

Our school also has been a pioneer in bringing its educational program into an internationally recognized Turkish university (Girne American University), and hence providing recognition with a certificate of acknowledgment for astrology education at the university level. Certificates are given and signed by the rectorate, and classes are held on university premises. This program started in 2014 and students should exhibit 75% eligibility in obtaining the certificate.

Apart from online web broadcasting, we have established our own publishing company to provide our own textbooks, and we have also liaised with international astrologers who provide their knowledge for Turkish readers, including Glenn Perry, Lea Imsiragic, Deborah Houlding, and Benjamin Dykes.

Our school is situated in Istanbul, which has been a bridge between Eastern and Western cultures for centuries. Hence, apart from teaching and distributing knowledge we have the vision to create an internationally recognized social environment for followers of astrology, sharing astrological developments on a worldwide scale. To that end, since 2012 we have organized the annual "International Astrology Days" in March at the spring equinox. Every year we provide a special discussion topic for our international guest speakers to elaborate on for the benefit of the public, in addition to seminars and workshops for astrology students. We publish the outcome as a separate volume.

International Astrology Days Activities in Istanbul (since 2012)

Our school is now a proud affiliate of ISAR (International Society for Astrological Research), through which it is now able to provide its students the opportunity to obtain an internationally recognized proficiency certificate for their astrology education. We believe that this is a great chance for students who want to enjoy a worldwide mutual understanding for their level of astrological knowledge, as well as being a member of a school whose name is amongst the top names of worldwide schools.

An ISAR-affiliated school offers advantages for expanding one's borders and liaise within a worldwide network which is constantly in tune with the current developments of astrological knowledge, as one of the prime purposes of the ISAR Affiliated School Program is to create an educational resource for astrologers worldwide. ISAR only recognizes those schools of astrology whose curriculum enables its students of astrology to acquire mutually accepted global standards of knowledge, contributing to a worldwide professional education.

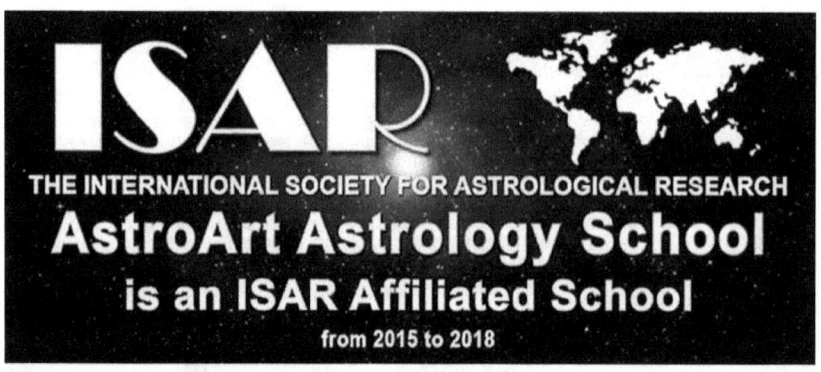

Students who wish to obtain an ISAR CAP (Certificate of Astrological Proficiency) certificate first should first complete our school's educational program and pass the exams with at least 70%, and then apply to ISAR CAP. ISAR requires proof of proficiency in three areas:

- ISAR Ethics training
- ISAR Consulting Skill training
- ISAR Competency Exam

Applicants who successfully complete those steps receive their ISAR CAP certificate, which is currently the highest certification in the world of astrology. Detailed further information can be obtained from the school's administration or from the link given below:

www.astrolojiokulu.com

We would hereby like to take the liberty to indicate our pleasure at being part of such a distinguished society, and emphasize our gratitude for those who helped us on that road. We also thank the community of ISAR directors for welcoming us, with special thanks to Alex Imsiragic who suggested and initiated the idea in the first place.

On Behalf of the AstroArt Astrology School Istanbul,
Öner Döşer, AMA, ISAR CAP
Director

Books Published in English by

ASTROART ASTROLOGY SCHOOL

Financial Significators
Öner Döşer

Marriage Significators
Öner Döşer

Professional Significators
Öner Döşer

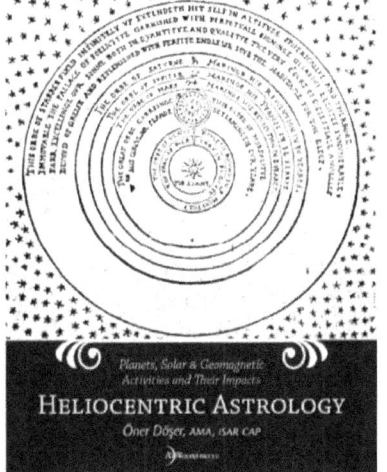

Heliocentric Astrology
Öner Döşer

Books Published in English by

ASTROART ASTROLOGY SCHOOL

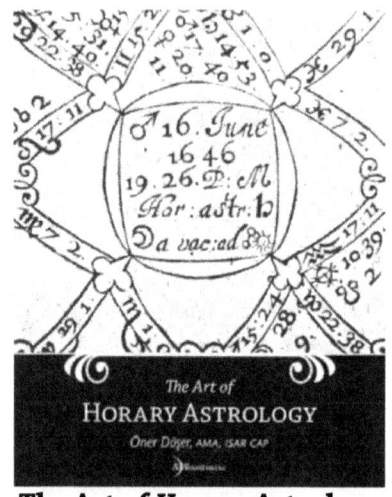

The Art of Horary Astrology
Öner Döşer

Karma, Fate, Free Will and Astrology
Öner Döşer

An Islamic View of Hermetic Knowledge
Öner Döşer

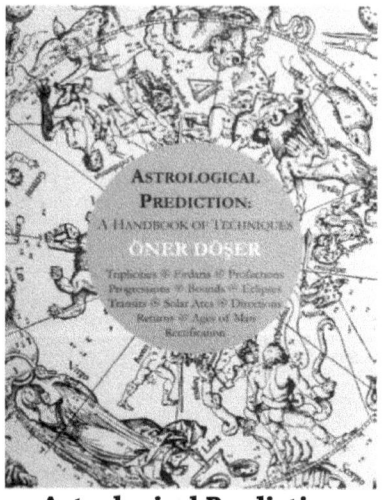

Astrological Prediction
Öner Döşer

www.ingramcontent.com/pod-product-compliance
Lightning Source LLC
Chambersburg PA
CBHW060513100426
42743CB00009B/1302